D1373477

THE
HORSE
NUTRITION
BIBLE

RUTH BISHOP

THE
HORSE
NUTRITION
BIBLE

THE COMPREHENSIVE
GUIDE TO THE CORRECT
FEEDING OF YOUR HORSE

David and Charles

A DAVID & CHARLES BOOK

David & Charles is a subsidiary of F+W (UK) Ltd.,
an F+W Publications Inc. company

First published in the UK in 2003
Reprinted 2004
First UK paperback edition 2005

Distributed in North America
by F+W Publications, Inc.
4700 E. Galbraith Rd.
Cincinnati, OH 45236
1-800-289-0963

ISBN 0 7153 1368 1 hardback
ISBN 0 7153 2209 5 paperback

Commissioning Editor: Jane Trollope
Art Editor: Sue Cleave
Copy Editor: Anne Plume
Production Controller: Ros Napper

Printed in Singapore by KHL
for David & Charles
Brunel House   Newton Abbot   Devon

Visit our website at www.davidandcharles.co.uk

David & Charles books are available from all good
bookshops; alternatively you can contact our
Orderline on 0870 9908222 or write to us at
FREEPOST EX2 110, D&C Direct, Newton Abbot,
TQ12 4ZZ (no stamp required UK mainland).

CONTENTS

Introduction	**6**
Digestive Physiology	8
1: The Ingredients of a Horse's Diet	**17**
The horse feed spectrum	18
Water	20
Forages	22
Grass	22
Hay	28
Haylage	30
Silage	32
Straw	33
Chaffs and hay replacers	34
Forage analysis	35
Straights	36
Cereals	36
Bran	38
Sugar-beet pulp	39
Linseed/full fat soya	40
Compound Feeds	42
Ingredients of compound feeds	44
GMOs and horse feeds	45
Supplements	46
Oil	47
Succulents	49
Nutrient supplements	49
Herbs	50
Digestive aids	50

2: Science into Practice: Feeding Principles — 53

Making the choice — 54
The rules of good feeding — 55
Calculating the basic ration — 60
Feeding for a contented horse — 62
Feed management — 64
Types of feed — 68
Choosing a product — 74

3: Problem Solver: Feeding to Requirement — 77

The horse feed year — 78
Feeding your first horse or pony — 80
Feeding the pony — 82
Feeding the excitable horse — 84
Feeding the competition horse — 86
Feeding the older horse or pony — 90
Feeding the brood mare — 92
Feeding the stallion — 96
Feeding youngstock — 98
Feeding the orphaned foal — 100
Feeding the racehorse — 102
Feeding box-resting horses — 104
Feeding to put condition on a horse — 106
Feeding to lose weight — 110

4: Diet-related Ailments and Feeding Myths — 113

Poor performance — 114
Colic — 116
Laminitis — 118

Equine Rhabdomyolosis Syndrome — 122
Gastric ulcers — 126
Allergies and intolerances — 128
Ailments associated with growth — 130
Choke — 132
Liver damage and disease — 134
Stereotypical behaviours — 136
Recurrent airway obstruction — 138
Common feeding myths — 140
Sugar in a horse's diet — 140
Feeding bran — 142
Performance boosters — 143

5: Nutrition Fundamentals — 145

Water — 146
Energy — 148
Carbohydrates — 150
Heating and non-heating — 154
Fats and oils — 156
Protein — 158
Minerals — 162
Antioxidants — 168
Vitamins — 170
Physiology in Perspective — 172
Exercise physiology — 174
Growth physiology — 176

Glossary — 178
Useful Addresses — 181
Conversion Table — 181
Index — 182

INTRODUCTION

You are what you eat, and so is your horse.

Feeding horses isn't about studying nutrition texts and reciting them to the letter, it's about developing an understanding of the ingredients of the horse's diet, and having confidence in what will and what won't work for the horse or horses in your care. Nothing is more pleasurable than the sound of contented munching coming from the stable.

Horses aren't like us; they don't 'do' fast food, go out for meals with friends, or snatch a quick bite sitting at their desks. For them, life is full of the security of their routine, their home patch, their circle of friends (which will include you), and the anticipation of the rustle of the haynet and the clatter of the food hitting the bucket. Your horse only ever whinnies at you when you're promising food, so make sure it's worth it.

In contrast to these simple pleasures for the horse, buying food for our horses can be an ordeal. Often making a purchase in a hurry, at your local feed store you are presented with hundreds of different products from which to choose. However, feeding your horse should be as pleasurable for you as it is for the horse, and this book is here to help you through the feeding maze. Use it as a hardback helpline that talks you through the areas to consider, with supporting background nutrition and science to give you the reasons that lie behind the advice.

First of all, however, it is useful to take an overall view of how the horse's digestive system has evolved, because the way it works still dictates how we feed our horses today.

An understanding of the natural

feeding habits of horses in the wild should shape our thinking about the way we feed domesticated horses

Digestive Physiology

The evolutionary horse was constantly on the move, covering large distances daily and selecting its food continuously from a varied mix of plants. Despite over 2,000 years of domestication, this lifestyle still shapes the digestive physiology of the modern horse, which remains best able to cope with that little-and-often kind of feeding. Owners frequently overlook the profound effect of gut design on the psychology of an animal used to eating at any time.

The whole digestive tract is a huge organ that accounts for about 15 per cent of a horse's total weight when full – and whilst we're all familiar with the phrase 'No hoof, no horse', which clearly conveys the message that if you don't look after the feet you have an unusable equine, there isn't a similar one for the digestive system, even though its sheer size indicates its obvious importance. Catchy phrases using the word 'gut' just don't spring to mind, and as a result, the feet seem generally to receive more attention.

The reason we feed our horses is to provide nutrients for routine body maintenance and to sustain the extra demands we ask from them. This process of digestion breaks down the feedstuffs into those sub-units that can be absorbed and utilized by the individual cells of the body. There are different sections of the digestive tract, each fulfilling a function to ensure this process is as efficient as it can be.

These mares and foals have their grazing supplemented with big-bale hay to which they have constant access

The Mouth

Whilst we use our hands to feed ourselves, our horses are equally nifty using their lips instead. There are plenty of horses well able to pick out the bits they don't like from their feed, right down to cunningly hidden medicinal powders.

The dental arcade of the horse consists of sharp biting teeth at the front, called the incisors, followed further up the jaw by the chewing and grinding teeth of the premolars and molars. Food is brought into the mouth either by the lips, or, in the case of forage, torn by the incisors. Food is then passed to the rear of the mouth for grinding by the molars. The rhythmical chomping sound that horses make when chewing is one of their signals of great contentment.

Breaking all the food down into tiny particles, typically less than 2mm, by grinding begins the process of digestion. Saliva is produced when the horse eats, and the process of chewing exposes the food to the saliva; thus the smaller the particles, the more thoroughly they will mix with saliva, which lubricates the bolus of food that passes down to the stomach.

DENTAL HYGIENE

Your horse needs to see a dentist as often as you do: with 40–42 teeth in its mouth, there is plenty of scope there for routine maintenance. If its teeth are in good order, not only can a horse extract maximum benefit from the food it eats, but it makes for a happy horse. Food improperly chewed may predispose a horse to conditions such as choke or colic. Sharp edges or hooks on molars that develop naturally as a result of their grinding action can cause pinching to the inside of the cheeks and tongue; in uncorrected cases, the upper molars can extend by as much as half a tooth over the lower teeth. Signs of an uncomfortable mouth are quidding (messy eating, with food being spilt from the mouth as the horse eats), and reluctance to eat.

The development of such hooks is in fact another artefact of modern horse husbandry. Feeding hay in a net, or feed from a raised manger, is to create an unnatural feeding position – horses are used to eating off the ground, and their jaw movements are different, depending

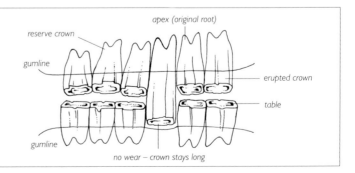

The loss of a tooth in the bottom jaw means that the opposing tooth could grow into the gap, stopping the backward and forward side-to-side jaw action

apex (original root)

reserve crown

gumline

erupted crown

table

gumline

no wear – crown stays long

Using a haynet produces an unnatural feeding position, which affects the wear on a horse's teeth

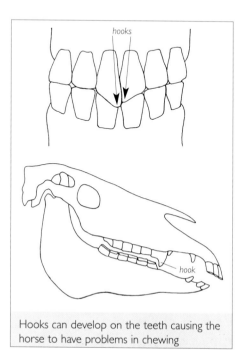

Hooks can develop on the teeth causing the horse to have problems in chewing

on the height at which they eat. Eating from floor level promotes a natural rotation of the jaw that seems to reduce the incidence of dental hooks.

The correctness of the teeth has far greater influence than on the digestion of feed alone. The horse's head is a very heavy part of the body suspended at the end of a long neck, and its jaw is a huge hinge that pivots from just behind the ears. This means that any discomfort in the mouth affects the hinge and the way the head is carried, and this in turn affects the whole way the horse goes. A horse that is unhappy in its mouth may go stiff through its back, toss its head more than normal, chew or play with the bit, or even buck.

The Stomach

The term 'stomach' is used regularly to describe the whole digestive tract, but this could not be more inaccurate in the case of the horse. In fact the stomach is small in comparison to the rest of the digestive tract, accounting for just 10 per cent of the digestive capacity. It works best when it is no more than two-thirds full, so its active capacity is therefore only 6 per cent of the total digestive capability.

The relatively small size of the stomach reflects the little-and-often way a horse evolved to receive its food, since a large stomach isn't necessary when food supply is constant. A quirk of this design, however, is that the horse's stomach produces acid continuously regardless of whether it contains any food or not. This is in contrast to the mouth, which only produces saliva when the horse chews. This continual production of stomach acid is thought to lie behind the development of gastric ulcers in some situations (see section 4).

The Small Intestine

Like the stomach, the small intestine is relatively small compared to the total digestive capacity of the horse, again reflecting its relative importance in the little-and-often, high-fibre diet of the horse.

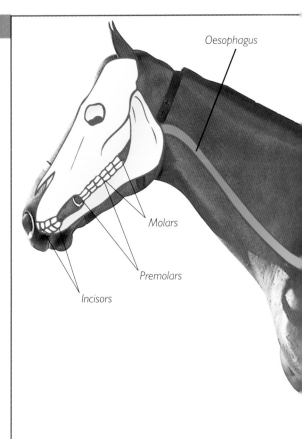

Oesophagus

Molars

Premolars

Incisors

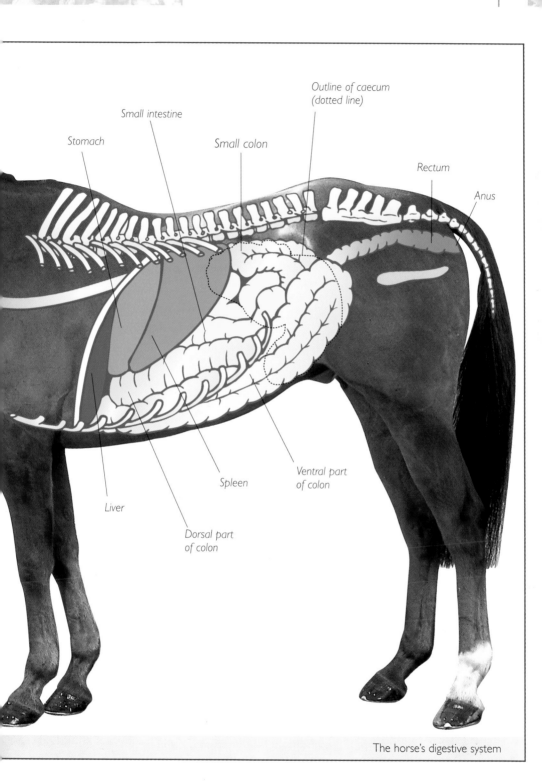

Outline of caecum
(dotted line)

Small intestine

Stomach

Small colon

Rectum

Anus

Liver

Spleen

Ventral part
of colon

Dorsal part
of colon

The horse's digestive system

The Large Intestine

No animal can digest fibre alone – it needs the help of a large microbial population to ferment it down into absorbable materials. Cattle, sheep and other ruminants do this in the rumen, one of their four stomachs, which acts as a fermentation vessel at the front end of their digestive tract. Horses also have the necessary fermenting capability, but at the rear end of their digestive tract, in the hindgut, or large intestine consisting of the colon and caecum. The site of this fermentation capacity appears related to the way in which they have evolved; for instance, the ancestors of cattle and sheep developed high digestive efficiency, but accepted that this meant travelling at slower speeds. Horses, on the other hand, opted for fast throughput of food, meaning that less of its nutritive value was extracted, but they were nimble enough to flee in times of dire need.

IN SUMMARY The horse's whole system relies on a continuous supply of food: for the modern horse, some sort of forage feed should be constantly on offer, and concentrates should be given in small amounts throughout the day. Leave him without some sort of food, and you may be causing the sort of psychological stress – manifested in weaving, crib-biting, box-walking, rug-chewing – that is equivalent to the potentially harmful physical effects of colic, choke and digestive upset. Many of these problems are a direct result of an inappropriate feeding regime.

Stomach statistics

Size	8 litres (14 pints) of liquid, comprising about 10 per cent of the digestive capacity of the horse.
Digests	Limited protein breakdown.
Method of digestion	Highly acidic conditions and enzymes begin the process of digestion but not much occurs.
What is absorbed here?	Nothing.
How long does this take?	Most food passes through quickly, but the stomach is rarely empty, with some food there for between two and six hours after a meal.

Small intestine statistics

Size	21–25m (69–82ft) long narrow tube holding about 20 per cent of the horse's digestive capacity, comprising three main parts: the duodenum (the part immediately after the stomach), the jejunum, and the ileum (the part immediately before the large intestine).
Digests	Starches, sugar, protein and oils.
Method of digestion	Enzymes.
What is absorbed here?	Sugars, amino acids, fatty acids, minerals, trace elements and vitamins A, D, and E.
How long does this process take?	This varies with the type of food, meal size offered and the amount of forage fed. It can take as little as 15 minutes for the first particles to pass through, but mostly it takes between 45 minutes and 2 hours.

Large intestine statistics

Size	This large fermentating organ comprises about two-thirds of the total digestive tract, and can hold up to 30 gallons (100 litres) of water and food.
Digests	Fibrous materials are fermented together with any other undigested matter from the small intestine, such as starch sugar and protein.
Method of digestion	Microbial fermentation.
What is absorbed here?	Water and some minerals, notably phosphorous, are absorbed, as are the volatile fatty acids and B vitamins generated by the microbial fermentation of fibre.
How long does this process take?	In horses receiving mostly hay or haylage this can be as long as 48 hours.
Large intestine disruption	The microbial population of the hindgut can adapt to match the kind of diet it receives, but this takes about 14 days. Any sudden changes do not allow sufficient time for adaptation and will cause digestive upset, as the bacteria present will be the 'wrong' ones to process the new feed. Such changes usually occur when starch and sugar overflow from the small intestine, for instance if hard feed is suddenly increased. This can be harmful to the horse (see Section 4 and table p.160).

1 Ingredients of a Horse's Diet

In this section

❑ The horse feed spectrum   18

❑ Water   20

❑ Forages   22
   Grass • Hay • Haylage • Silage • Straw •
   Chaffs and hay replacers • Forage analysis

❑ Straights   36
   Cereals • Bran • Sugar-beet pulp •
   Linseed/full fat soya

❑ Compound Feeds   42
   Cubes • Mixes • Balancers • Ingredients of
   compound feeds

❑ Supplements   46
   Oil • Succulents • Vitamin and mineral supplements •
   Herbs • Treats • Digestive Aids

The Horse Feed Spectrum

Walk into any store and the dietary options on offer are many and varied. This is in complete contrast to the best feeding advice, which is to keep it simple. Most horses will eat any feeds offered, even those that are not good for it. This chapter discusses all the feeds commonly available and their nutritive values to horses, starting with the fibre providers (that is, the equivalent of roughage), and finishing up with a look at all of those extras that we commonly add to their diets.

Every one of the hundreds of feeds available belong at some point on the following spectrum, whether they're fed in large or small quantities:

Forages	Chaffs	Fibre mixes	Cubes	Coarse mixtures (sweet feeds)	Straights	Balancers	Supplements	Treats
Fed in large quantities							Fed in small quantities	

Feed Spectrum Analysed

❑ Forages encompass the ingredients that supply roughage and form the greatest part of most horses' diets, fed in kilos per day.

❑ Chaffs have broadly the same nutritional value as forages, but are often considered and used as an addition to the hard feed rather than as forage replacers. Usually blends of chopped straw and molasses, or sometimes blends of chopped alfalfa or grass, and straw, mixed with molasses, are used to add bulk to the bucket or hard feed, to slow down the rate of consumption. Chaffs are usually fed in double handfuls, equivalent to a matter of grams per day.

❑ Fibre mixes are the most recent entrant in the competition for shelf space in store, and combine the physical form of chaff with the added nutrition of a compound.

❑ Cubes, the original form of compound horse feed, are still widely popular.

❑ Coarse mixtures or mueslis (sweet feeds), mixtures of flakes and pellets, lightly covered in a molasses or other coating, are equally popular to cubes.
  All three forms (fibre mixes, cubes and coarse mixtures) supply energy, protein, vitamins and minerals in the diets of working horses, and are fed at anything from 1kg to 8kg (2.2lb to 17.6lb) per day.

❑ Balancers are also relatively new to the horse feed repertoire, and sit between traditional compounds and supplements. These provide concentrated nutrients in usually a pellet form, and are fed at rates about halfway between compounds and supplements.

❑ Supplements are low dose (50–100g (1.8–3.5oz) per day), functional extras added to the diet.

❑ Treats are just as their name suggests, the equivalent of sweets and biscuits as a reward or greeting for your horse.

Water

Water is often the most overlooked, but in fact the most essential ingredient of a horse's diet. Strangely, drinking water from a bucket, trough or watercourse is not always essential for survival, as there is some water in all feedstuffs. For instance, a horse grazing lush spring grass can meet all its requirements from the grass alone, on the other hand a stabled horse with no access to grass will certainly require extra water. Stabled horses require clean, fresh, uncontaminated water to be provided frequently.

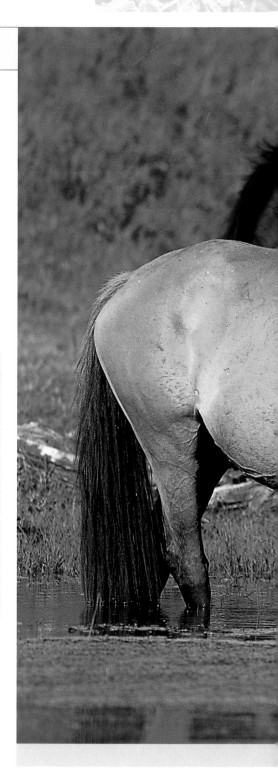

The water content of feedstuffs		
Feed	Water content	Dry matter
Carrots	90	10%
Grass	80	20%
Soaked sugar-beet pulp	80	20%
Haylage	35	65%
Oats	15	85%
Hay	15	85%
Coarse mixes (sweet feeds)	14	86%
Cubes	13	87%
Dry sugar-beet pulp	12	88%

Water might contain traces of minerals, but it has no energy or protein value, and so its presence in a feedstuff dilutes the supply of nutrients per kilo. One kilo of hay will always contain more energy and protein than one kilo of haylage, as the latter contains more water.

A constant supply of uncontaminated water is the most important ingredient of the horse's diet

Forages

Horses rely on the forage part of their diet to provide the roughage necessary for a healthy digestive tract. Forage is usually green and bulky, and generally considered uninteresting by the horse owner, but it does form the greatest part of most horses' diets. In fact it is often overlooked when owners describe the contents of their horse's diet. They list the compounds and the supplements, and forget the forage.

Grass

Most people's idea of perfect pasture is that smooth, even, green grassland in Newmarket or Kentucky grazed by elegant Thoroughbred mares and stallions, and their cheeky but expensive foals. This is grass doing what grass undoubtedly does best: providing a deeply nutritious feed and exercise system, rolled into one.

Good pasture has an even cover of palatable grasses, is free from weeds, and is without the defined 'lawns' and 'roughs' that arise when horses continually graze in one area and dung in another.

Some pastures are well kept, others may be weed infested and horse-sick. However, the same general principles apply to grass whatever the quality.

Grass is at its very richest in spring, when the protein content can be up as high as 28 per cent, and the energy content equivalent to that of a competition feed. Of the sources of energy, sugar is the main contributor, with up to 5 per cent of every intake in this form; this is very good for mares with foals, but too good for other horses (see p.140 'Sugar in a horse's diet'). These actual values won't apply to poor quality pasture, but even with values half these, a horse will still receive more from its pasture than it will from most low-energy feeds.

Not only is spring grass exceedingly nutritious, it also grows about five times faster in May than it does in September. Well managed paddocks, supporting three to four horses per acre in spring, will be providing nutrients equal to 10kg (22lb) per day of medium energy feed to each horse. The springtime onslaught of rapidly growing, highly nutritive grass is the main reason for the accelerated weight gain and laminitis often seen at this time.

When making diets for horses at grass, it is often difficult to estimate the amount of grass eaten, and therefore the total energy supply of the horse. The following is a guide to intakes:

Nutritive value

The amount of nutrition that grass is capable of providing varies according to the:
- ❑ time of year;
- ❑ general standard of upkeep of the grazing
- ❑ number of horses (or other animals) grazing the land.

Hours at grass	Typical intake (kg/day)	Check
1hr	10kg (22lb) grass fresh weight, equivalent to 2kg (4.5lb) dry matter.	Quality of grass. Does the horse eat or move around.
Out during day, or during night only	Assume 50–60% of daily intake is grass. For the 500kg (1,100lb) horse, this is equivalent to: 500 × 2% × 50% = 5kg (11lb) of grass dry matter, or 25kg (55lb) of fresh weight.	Quality of grass: shorter, grazed-down grass will not provide as much to eat.
All the time	Assume 100% of daily intake is grass. For a 500kg horse this is equivalent to 500 × 2% ×100% = 10kg (22lb) of grass dry matter, or 50kg (110lb) grass fresh weight.	Quality of grass

Mixed grazing provides a natural method of parasite control and more even cropping overall

Grassland Management

In the daily routine of horse care and management there is often little time to give grass serious consideration; most people use it only for turnout, demand little nutrition from it, and so do very little to look after it – and looking after it does take time. However, it is unwise to ignore your grass, as turning a blind eye won't make problems go away, and there are plenty of rough-looking, horse-sick pastures to be found as a result.

The major issues in managing grazing are soil damage through poaching and under-grazing the grass available.

POACHING occurs when horses are turned out on to wet pastures – sometimes unavoidably. Their hooves cut through the grass, the top layer of soil and into the subsoil beneath, and this not only creates mud, but also damages the soil structure, which both affects the soil's ability to drain and encourages weed growth. These opportunist weeds are the first to colonize the resulting bare soil. Poaching can be repaired by treading divots, and rolling. Rolling has to be done when the soil is soft but not wet – if paddocks are too wet, the tractor and roller will cause more damage than repair; conversely, rolling will achieve nothing if the soil is too dry.

UNDER-GRAZING occurs when the horses in a field cannot eat it down at the same rate at which it grows. Grass does not grow at the same rate throughout the year: the rate is low in winter, high in spring and early summer. It drops off during the heat of the summer, followed by an autumn flush, usually in September. A good rule of thumb is that the grass grows when the soil temperature is above 5°C. Forget the general rule of one acre per horse, as it doesn't cater for this variation. In May, good grazing will feed about three to four 16hh horses per acre, or five to six 13hh ponies. In September, one acre will support one horse or two ponies at most, and not even that if the grazing is poor.

Horses become choosy about what they eat when there's too much grass. Two situations then arise: first, the grass that is ungrazed grows long and runs to seed, allowing the invasion of weeds and species of grass that are less palatable to horses. Second, horses choose not to eat where they dung and urinate, and as a result the paddock becomes a combination of heavily grazed areas of short grass that may not provide enough grazing and are prone to hoof damage, and others where grass is overlong and unpalatable. Up to half the potential grazing area can be lost in this way.

WEEDS In a recent survey of pastures in the UK, 80 per cent of pastures that were poached were found to be infested with weeds. The most common weeds of horse pastures are thistles, docks, buttercups, nettles and ragwort. As they invade as a result of under-management, any effort to spray or pull them without altering management practices only provides a short-term solution. Creating a dense mat of grass through regular topping or hard grazing both suffocates weeds, and prevents horses from receiving excess grass.

Management falls into two categories: first damage limitation and then active improvement, and both take time to achieve results.

Doing nothing isn't an option – grassland will deteriorate otherwise.

Droppings should be cleared on a regular basis to keep pasture sweet

'Bare minimum' grassland management

- ❏ 'mend' poaching damage;
- ❏ pick up droppings;
- ❏ control excess growth by topping or grazing;
- ❏ remove weeds.

'Active' grassland improvement

- ❏ **Analyse the soil:** Soil tests are a cheap and easy way to assess the basic ability of the soil to provide nutrients for the grass to grow.
- ❏ **Fertilize:** This is not a dirty word, although many horse owners are wary of using it. Grass needs food to grow, as much as a horse does. Of course, too much can cause problems through stimulating too much grass growth, but for grazing only, about 30kg (66lb)/hectare of nitrogen provides growth without abundance.
- ❏ **Control grass height:** Keep grass at 7–8cm (3in) in height by topping, or by increasing the number of animals grazing, be they sheep, cattle or horses.
- ❏ **Pick up droppings:** The grass will be tainted if droppings are left for more than twenty-four hours. One horse produces on average eight lots of droppings per day – going out daily should mean an easy barrow to push.
- ❏ **Kill weeds:** It's not as easy as just spraying them. Control through pulling, cutting and spraying alongside improved management that excludes them, will remove weeds and keep them away.
- ❏ **Reseed:** If the pasture has deteriorated so much that new grasses are needed, think about reseeding. Improved grassland through slot seeding or over-sowing will be better able to withstand hoof damage than young, newly sown complete reseeds. Beware of clover in a reseed – even if added at 5 per cent or less, it can spread and take over the whole pasture.

Grassland management and the laminitic horse

Those with ponies or horses that are highly susceptible to laminitis may feel that grass is not compatible with them. Grassland management cannot be ignored, but laminitics do not need much grass, particularly between April and September. Such animals' intakes of grass should be limited, by turning out into a bare paddock, or offering stabled, at-risk animals forage in the form of hay, and the use of feeds that are high in fibre, and low in starch and sugar.

Topping pastureland to control the grass height

Hay

The invention of hay in the early part of the first millennium has been credited with changing the world. Until then, horses were only used to any great extent in those parts of the world where grass was permanently available. But hay meant that horses could be used all year round in areas where grass growth varied with the seasons, for instance in northern Europe, and this allowed man to travel further and do battle more effectively.

Despite this romantic past, less and less hay is grown. The ease of making haylage, and the poor hay-making conditions often found in temperate climates such as the UK, make hay a less attractive crop. Other countries with better drying weather, such as America and Canada, still continue to make good hay, which is often imported into damper countries for feeding to racehorses.

Hay is grass that is cut and dried in the summer months and then stored for use in the winter when grass is not available. The grass is dried to a moisture content below which mould does not develop, allowing it to be stored under cover, but without wrapping or packaging the individual bales. Hay falls into two general categories: seed hay and meadow hay.

Soaking hay

Very little of the hay grown in damper climes, such as northern Europe or Britain, is dust free, the dust consisting mainly of mould spores from field or barn spoilage. As a result it is common practice to soak it. Soaking hay causes the dust or spores either to be washed off, or to swell and stick to the grass stalks, thus meaning they are ingested rather than inhaled. Soaking is tedious; it requires large amounts of water and a bin in which to soak the hay; in the winter, the water can be frozen, and it is downright unpleasant to manhandle cold wet hay; in the summer the water quickly becomes brackish, as the nutrients that have leached into it turn it into an odiferous effluent. Water in which hay has been soaked shouldn't be poured down the drain or into watercourses, since technically it is a powerful pollutant.

How long to soak

Some people steam their hay for ten minutes, others soak it for twenty-four hours, and within these extremes lies the optimum. The purpose is either to remove the spores from the grass, or cause them to stick to it. Research has shown that thirty minutes soaking achieves this, although sometimes it fits in better in the day to soak a net in the morning for use at night, and vice versa. Bear in mind, too, that a certain amount of the soaked hay's nutritional value will be lost as some soluble sugars and proteins are leached out into the water.

Horse owners are less concerned with the nutritive value of their hay than with its hygienic quality. Hay has to dry for about three days in the field before it is dry enough to bale – this can be a long time in a temperate climate. Hay that becomes wet while lying in the field will develop certain moulds, and whilst these won't necessarily cause disease, if present in sufficient number they can cause a respiratory allergy if fed in a poorly ventilated stable. Hay that is baled slightly damp, or that is not stored correctly after baling, is of greater concern because it can heat up during storage as a result of microbial activity. The resulting moulds are those that can thrive in the horse's respiratory tract, such as *Aspergillus fumigatus*. This mould is linked to the development of chronic obstructive pulmonary disease (COPD) or recurrent airway obstruction in horses, and farmer's lung in humans (see Section 4, Diet-Related Ailments).

An important feature of hay, and to a lesser extent haylage consumption, is the amount of water associated with them in the digestive tract. For every kilo of hay eaten, 2.5–3.5kg (5½–8lb) of water is bound with it. This occurs as a result of the chewing and mixing of the forage particles with saliva and digestive secretions, that is not then easily released for absorption. This fluid acts as an internal fluid reservoir for the horse.

Seed hay

Seed hay is made from grass mixtures specially grown for hay production. Italian or perennial ryegrasses, Timothy and specialist blends of them, are all commonly available forms of seed hay. It generally tends to be quite coarse in nature, with a relatively low nutritive value.

Meadow hay

This is cut from permanent pasture, and usually comprises a more varied mixture of grass species than that specially sown. Generally, meadow hay has a higher nutritive value than seed hay.

Haylage

The availability of haylage as a specialist preserved forage for horses has exploded since the first such product, HorseHage, appeared on the market in the 1980s. Haylage is a cross between hay and silage, where grass is grown and cut similarly to hay, but baled before it is dry, generally when there is about 35–40 per cent of the moisture remaining. To prevent mould spoilage, it is then bagged or wrapped, like silage, to keep air out. It is easier to make because it does not need three or four days to dry in the field, and the airtight seal renders the mould and dust presence very low. Often the nutritive value of haylage is slightly higher than hay. On the down side, horses find it very palatable as it is moister and tends to contain more sugar than hay. Thus horses can devour it more quickly than they do hay, meaning the haylage-fed horse may suffer boredom, put on weight, or both. Competitors find small bale haylage useful as it can travel on top of the lorry without spoiling. All haylage, being covered in polythene, can be stored outside.

Using haylage

❏ Feed about 1½ times the weight of haylage as hay: up to 50 per cent of haylage can be water, compared to some 15 per cent in hay, so it cannot be fed on a weight-for-weight basis with hay. It may appear a large amount, but it will prevent digestive disturbances through feeding too little fibre.

❏ The quality of the airtight seal is essential. Air ingress will allow mould growth in the bales, since wrapping merely halts microbiological activity, rather than destroying it. Check small bales for splits at the seal and elsewhere, and that large bales are covered with preferably eight layers of plastic, to prevent the fibrous haylage stalks from penetrating through. Check the wrap or bag before feeding for holes from bird, rodent or mole damage.

❏ Always buy haylage from a reputable manufacturer. Quality is all-important, so choose a company with a reputation for making quality haylage, and ask them for an analysis of their product. Such companies will also have product liability insurance if the worst happens and their product makes your horse ill.

❏ Always use a bale within four days of opening (less in summer), as moulds start to grow again immediately the bale is opened.

❏ Avoid feeding visibly mouldy haylage where the airtight seal has not been effective. Avoid also haylage that feels 'gritty' or is soil contaminated, as there could be a risk to you and your horse of listeriosis.

❏ Many owners worry about botulism, but the likelihood of this occurring in haylage is minute since the organism that causes the disease, *Clostridium botulinum*, only survives in very wet silages, and not at the moisture contents seen in haylages. Horses are more likely to suffer colic associated with feeding haylage.

HorseHage, the original haylage and (inset) being fed from a haynet

Silage

If the aim of growing forage for horses is to provide the 'munch factor', along with low energy nutrition. Silage is made for completely different reasons. To a farmer, grass and silage are his cheapest feed, and he aims to get the most nutrition from it; hence farm-grown big-bale silage is much higher in energy and protein than horse forages. Big bales also tend to be wetter. Whereas dry haylages tend to be almost vacuum packed, silage undergoes a fermentation or 'pickling' of the grass in the bale, where the moisture, plant sugars and naturally occurring bacteria in the grass combine to produce lactic acid. Such a fermentation is not necessarily harmful to the horse, if it successfully preserves the bale, but a poor fermentation in a wet silage can cause problems and in the worst case can lead to botulism. It is for these reasons that feeding big bale silage to horses is not recommended.

Big-bale silage: much higher in energy than other forages but carries the risk of botulism

Straw

Straw is not often used as a forage in the UK, but in continental Europe it is often expected that a horse will consume a proportion of its straw bed each day as part of its daily diet. Straw as such is not bad for horses, but then again, it is not necessarily sufficiently nutritious (low energy, low protein). However, there are many horses and ponies that do not need high levels of energy or protein, and for these types straw is more than adequate as a source of roughage if necessary.

There are three kinds of straw: oat, barley and wheat. Good quality oat or barley straw is a useful alternative if seed hay or haylage are hard to get hold of, either as a total or partial replacer. Wheat straw is not usually used as a horse forage. Make sure, however, that any straw fed is as dust free as possible: straw is subject to the same kind of mould risks as hay.

Summary of Forage Feed Values

Forage	Bale size	Water content %	EnergyMJ/kg (dry weight)	Protein %	Calcium g/kg	Phosphorus g/kg	Trace elements	Vitamins
Grass	n/a	80-90	11–13	16–28	6	3	Copper and selenium marginal, zinc, manganese, iron, in excess	Rich
Meadow hay	Small, rectangular: 20kg (44lb); large, round/ square 300kg (660lb)	12–15	8–10	8–10	4-6	1.5–2.5	as Grass	Lacking in vitamin A/ beta-carotene Limited vitamin E activity
Seed hay	as Meadow Hay	12–15	5–8	4–7	4.6	1.5–2.5	as Grass	as Meadow Hay
Haylage	Small, vacuum packed: 25kg (55lb) large, round or square, wrapped: 180–250kg (400–550lb)	30–40	6–10	6–10	4.6	1.5–2.5	as Grass	as Meadow Hay
Silage	Large round bales: 300–400kg (660–880lb)	60–80	10–11	9–13	4.6	1.5–2.5	as Grass	as Meadow Hay
Barley straw	Small bales 20kg (44lb), large square/ round bales 350kg (770lb)	88–90	4–6	4–6			Low	as Meadow Hay

Chaffs and Hay Replacers

A number of products based on forage are available that provide quality roughage in a chopped, pre-packed form. They are marketed as forage replacers or chops and chaffs, to be added into the hard feed to slow down the rate of eating. As a result of their short chop length, they are best offered in a bucket or manger. There is some evidence to show that horses take longer to eat short chop forages than they do hay or haylage.

Different chaff types

Chaff type	Main ingredients	Suitable for	Energy	Protein
Molassed chaffs	Straw, molasses	All horses and ponies as a ration bulker	Low	Low (5–7%)
Forage blends	Straw, alfalfa and molasses	All horses and ponies as a ration bulker or as a hay replacer	Low	Medium (8–10%)
Pure grass or alfalfa	All grass or all alfalfa or a mixture of these and molasses	Competition horses, to slow the rate of feeding and add a small amount of extra fibre	Medium	High (15–18%)

Two types of chaff: (left) molassed chop and (right) dried alfalfa

Forage Analysis

Even though forage constitutes the largest part of most horses' diets, we often prefer to focus our feed decisions on which compound or which supplement to feed. However, forage feed value will have a greater effect on the horse than any other part of its diet, and analysis of the forage is relatively inexpensive.

Where to get it analysed

Many feed companies will arrange for this to be done, and local agricultural merchants might offer the same service.

What to ask for

❑ **Dry matter:** gives an indication of the moisture content of the sample.

❑ **Crude protein:** indicates the protein level in the forage.

❑ **Minerals:** only really necessary for performance horses (calcium, phosphorus, magnesium and sodium) and youngstock (copper, zinc, manganese and selenium).

❑ **For haylages:** pH, ammonia nitrogen and ash measure the quality of the preservation within the bale, and the effectiveness of the seal.

❑ **Mould count**

❑ **Mould identification:** some moulds are more harmful than others, even at relatively low levels – an analysis will identify any problems. Note that these are essential if a horse is in any kind of athletic work, or if you suspect your hay or haylage is dusty.

Making sense of the results

Whatever the results, they are only ever useful if they are made relevant to your feeding situation. Good nutritionists will be able to do this.

Straights

Straights are defined as feed ingredients available for purchase individually, rather than mixed and blended in proprietary feeds. At one time, before the advent of compound feeds, all horses were fed straights, and owners with a traditionalist streak still like to make up their own ration by adding scoops of these to their horses' diets. Do not, however, rely on these ingredients to contribute large amounts of vitamins and minerals to the diet; heavy use of these will in fact require balancing supplements.

Cereals

Cereals, along with sugar-beet pulp, are most commonly added to the feed bucket. Oats remain the most popular for adding some 'zip' to a horse, whilst barley and to a lesser extent maize are generally fed to add condition. In all cases the main nutrient added to the diet by cereals is starch.

OATS might not be the most energy-dense cereal around, but their continuing popularity stems from the fact that they are the traditional energy source for horses. This is most likely as a result of their being the safest of the cereals, containing the lowest starch and highest fibre content of them all.

Oats are traditionally fed rolled, a process that breaks open the husk (outer layer) of the oat, and allows the digestive enzymes easier access to the starch and other nutrients within.

Whole oats

Rolled oats

BARLEY AND MAIZE may be either flaked or micronized, both of which are 'cooking' processes designed to cook the starch within the cereal and make it more digestible. 'Flaking' involves cooking the cereal in steam to improve the digestibility, and then rolling the hot soft cereal into a flake. 'Micronizing' means cooking the cereal in infra-red heat, that is, grilling it and then rolling. Barley can also be fed boiled, a truly traditional method; it is mainly used as a method of improving condition in a horse.

Whole barley

Cereal Starch Content	
Cereal	Starch content %
Oats	**50**
Barley	**60**
Maize	**70**

Bruised barley

Flaked maize

Boiled barley

Bran

Bran is the outer husk of the wheat grain. Changes in the flour milling process mean it is not as 'broad' as it used to be, but it is still available albeit in a more mealy form. Commonly used in bran mashes, and to bulk out a ration, it was very popular as a cheap, high fibre, low starch, safe product to give to horses. It does, however, have a high phosphorous level, and needs to be balanced with added calcium (limestone) or a broad spectrum supplement. The protein quality is poor, and it has fairly low vitamins and minerals. (See also p.142 'Feeding Bran: What are the benefits?'.)

Recipe for a bran mash

Smell that delicious sweet aroma of a proper bran mash: you can't believe it's doing anything but good, or maybe it's just comfort food for sick or tired horses.

- ❑ Take about a third of a bucket of bran (this weighs approximately 3lb (1.3kg)), and add a good handful of salt.
- ❑ Add boiling water – as much as the bran absorbs, but remember that a mash should be crumbly, not sloppy in texture.
- ❑ Add some molasses to make it extra tasty (some people prefer to add a level scoop of oats).
- ❑ Stir well and cover.
- ❑ When cooled slightly, but still warm (usually after about 15–20 minutes), serve.

Bran

Sugar-beet Pulp

Sugar-beet pulp is probably the most frequently added 'extra' in horses' diets. Very wet or sloppy scoopfuls are mixed in with the rest of the hard feed to make a tasty, moist addition to the daily ration.

Sugar-beet pulp comes from sugar beet, and is a by-product from the extraction of sugar from sugar beet. It is high in digestible fibre, with an energy content similar to oats, and a good calcium content (from the addition of limestone during the extraction process).

The energy comes predominantly from fibre and sugar – molasses is added back into the pulp during processing to increase its palatability (although in today's sugar-fearing world, unmolassed – and therefore less tasty – beet pulp is available). Its sweetness, similar to the sugar content of spring grass, is what makes it such a popular appetizer.

Dried sugar-beet pulp will absorb water to twice its original volume. The fear of a ruptured stomach, colic or choke means

Sugar-beet facts

❏ 13% fibre, 23% sugar and high energy.

❏ Soaked sugar-beet pulp, added as one sloppy scoop per feed, only delivers about 500g (1.1lb) of the dry material, and contributes about 6MJ of energy (about 6% of a horse's daily calories), 65g (2.3oz) of fibre, and 110g (3.9oz) of sugar.

❏ As with soaked hay, in summer soaked sugar-beet pulp soon starts to ferment, and should be used within twenty-four hours.

Soaked sugar beet

that, in the UK at least, horse owners feed sugar-beet pulp that has been soaked for several hours, for instance overnight. In America however, sugar-beet pulp is fed dry, and some proprietary feeds contain high proportions of sugar-beet pulp, which are eaten without apparent ill-effect.

Sugar-beet pulp is often advocated for poor doers (difficult keepers). Although at typical feed rates its effect will be marginal, it does have a good energy content that comes principally from fibre and sugar, which are more natural energy sources for the horse.

Unsoaked sugar beet cubes

Raw linseed

Linseed and Full Fat Soya

Whole linseed and soya provide a slug of both protein and oil, and are sometimes used to add condition in horses. Not only are they highly calorific, the oil content of both are such that the horse's coat will look fantastic also. It's an expensive way of adding oil however, especially as both these protein sources contain anti-nutritional factors that require them to be cooked before they are fed. Linseed is traditionally cooked by boiling to a thick soup, whereas whole soya beans are usually toasted or micronized.

Whole soya beans must not be confused with the soya bean meal used as a feed

Linseed mash

❑ Soak a mugful (500–750g) (3.5–25.7oz) of linseed grains overnight, then boil hard for 10–20min to kill off the hydrocyanic acid that is the poisonous principle.

❑ Simmer until a jelly forms, usually overnight or throughout the day (don't let it boil dry).

❑ Feed. A scoopful mixed with the daily feed will add 100–150g oil (3.5–5.2oz) (equivalent to the usual glug from a bottle of oil) and 125g (4.39oz) of protein.

❑ Some people prefer to separate the jelly from the linseed mash, and to feed it with a bran mash.

ingredient; this material has had the oil extracted, whole soya beans have not, and have a greater oil content as a result.

Straight feed values

Straight	Moisture %	EnergyMJ/kg	Protein %	Ca g/kg	Pg/kg
Oats	12–15	11–12	9–12	0.7	3
Barley	12–15	12–13	9–10	0.6	3.3
Maize	12–15	13–15	8–9	0.2	3
Bran	10–15	10–11	13–15	1	12
Sugar-beet pulp	88–90 dry, 15–25, soaked or boiled	11 – 12	9–11	6	1
Linseed	As sugar-beet pulp	20	25–30	2.4	5.2
Full fat soya	10–12	20	25–30	3	6

Sugar beet in its various forms

Compound Feeds

A compound feed is a balanced blend of ingredients formulated to produce a complete ration that is easy to feed (in conjunction with forage for horses). Their one big advantage is that they are always nutritionally the same for a given feed, whereas straights are more variable.

Cubes, those little brown nuggets of goodness, were the original compound horse feed. Coarse mixes (sweet feeds) increased in popularity in the early 1980s, as owners showed a preference for these open, colourful mixes over cubes, which, given their uniformity of colour and size, were (and still are) often perceived as boring. It is the manufacturing process that renders cubes uniformly brown – and it is definitely not true, certainly amongst the leading brands, that poor quality ingredients are hidden in them. Moreover,

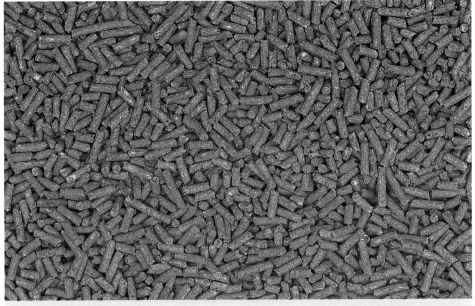

Foal and yearling pellets

Feed	Main ingredients	Typical feed rate
Low energy cube	Fibre sources	1–4kg (2–9lb)/day
Competition mix	Flaked cereals, rolled oats	2–6kg (4–14lb)/day
Racehorse cube	Cereals, protein sources, oils	5–7kg (11–15lb)/day
Feed balancers	Proteins, cereals	250–1,000g (1–2lb)/day

Compound feed

Coarse mix

coarse mixtures are not necessarily better than cubes just because you can see what is in them – in fact all that you really see are the flakes, as coarse mixes are a combination of flakes and ubiquitous pellets, the latter being necessary to carry the nutrients required by the horse, which are absent in the flakes.

Different feeds have different proportions of a common group of ingredients in them, depending on their design and purpose, and they are designed to be fed at different rates.

Ingredients are sourced directly from farms (in the case of cereals), from farm processors (grass or alfalfa), or from the human food industry. By-products from

Why are cubes brown?

Their colour comes from the base ingredients, which are mostly light brown in colour. Mixing up a cube recipe is rather like making a giant cake, although the size of the mixer is obviously much greater than the one in your kitchen. Instead of using eggs to bind the ingredients together as in a cake, horse feed manufacturers use molasses or treacle, another brown-coloured material that enhances the brownness further.

the production of sugar (molasses and sugar-beet pulp), flour milling (wheatfeed and oatfeed) or oil (soya products and sunflower meals), whilst not required for humans, make excellent ingredients for

Horse and pony nuts

What goes into Compound Feeds

Energy souces
Barley, wheat, oats, maize, molasses.

Fibres
Dried grass (usually pelleted) or lucerne, wheatfeed, oatfeed, soya hulls, sugar-beet pulp and straw.

Proteins
Soya-bean meal and sunflower meal.

Minerals/vitamins
Limestone, salt and trace mineral and vitamin premixes.

horses, with their completely different digestive systems.

Horse feed company nutritionists formulate first to meet the nutrient specification that is required of the feed, then for palatability and consistency of ingredients, next to avoid prohibited substances, and finally for cost. The so-called 'least cost' practice of formulation, as practised in the wider animal feed industry, does not happen in horse feed production, certainly amongst the leading manufacturers.

GMOs and Horse Feeds

GMO stands for 'genetically modified organism'. In the feed industry it describes seeds, and therefore crops, that have been manipulated by man to enhance or insert genes to produce characteristics that are not present following normal plant breeding and crossing (hybridization). These characteristics are often linked to disease or pesticide resistance.

In the USA most maize is grown using GM seed. In the EU, some GM maize has been cleared for use. The minor risk of cross-contamination has been recognized, so up to 1 per cent GM material is permitted in crops described as non-GM. Therefore manufacturers buying non-GM ingredients are advised to say feeds are made 'To the best of our knowledge without the use of GM ingredients', rather than 'GM free'. Currently, no GM cereals are permitted

to be grown commercially in the UK. The varieties of maize that produce the required yellow grains do not grow in the UK climate and are imported from the USA or France.

Identity Preserved (IP)

(IP) describes ingredients that are traceable back to their farm of origin and offers a degree of security that they are non-GM. Companies marketing non-GM horse feeds typically use IP soya and maize to achieve this.

The GM status of horse feeds usually arises where a horse owner wishes to sell his horse manure to an organic farm. To do this and maintain organic status, the organic farmer seeks an assurance from the owner, and therefore the feed company, that the feeds being used are non-GM. In fact this is somewhat arbitrary, because there is no such stipulation for the bedding materials that comprise the greatest part of horse manure.

Supplements

Supplements are best described as substances included in the diet in small quantities, giving, as their name suggests, a supplementary nutrient or substance in addition to those provided by the main part of the diet.

Be realistic about what a supplement can achieve. Good horsemastership comes first: thus a horse that does not hold its weight well could benefit from a visit from the dentist, a good worming, and more hard feed (some horses in poor condition do not actually receive much hard feed), or a horse that is excitable may thrive on cubes rather than a mix, or at least a low starch diet, before the tub of 'calm balm' comes out. Also, there is a limit to what nutrient supplementation at 100g per day or so can achieve when a horse's total intake is around 10kg per day. If the gross components of the diet aren't balanced, no amount of additives are going to fix it.

However, there are occasions when they can have an effect; so reach for the supplement tub if the following criteria apply:

❏ Less than 30 per cent of the total diet is compound feed, as hay and haylage do not supply sufficient vitamins and minerals alone.

❏ Straights form the large part of the hard feed, again as vitamins and minerals will be in short supply, especially calcium and vitamin E.

❏ The horse's condition and temperament are such that only very small amounts of hard feed are fed.

❏ Hay and haylage form the largest part of the diet. These contain only small amounts of vitamins A, D and E, so stabled horses require an extra supply, either from hard feed or from supplements.

❏ The grazing is horse sick, or in areas where it is known that certain soils are deficient in nutrients.

❏ Horses are fed only small amounts of forage.

Oil

Oil in the form of vegetable oils can be added as an energy supplement or for coat condition. It is ironic that oil, usually associated with all that is bad in human nutrition, is looked upon as something of a good thing in our horses' diets. The reason is twofold: first, it is well known for putting a shine on a horse's coat; and second, as a source of energy it is one of the alternatives that can replace starch in the diets of horses for which that nutrient is an issue, whether it is for temperamental or metabolic reasons.

Oil alone will not solve everything. For example, it contains 'empty' calories, containing no other nutrients. Feeding large amounts (ie over 1kg) will mean that a horse will put on weight, and recently published research suggests high intakes of oil may affect the digestion of fibre. So for diets where starch is wanted out, a combination of fibre and oil is better than oil alone.

Oil Facts

❑ How much oil can a horse eat? Researchers have pushed fat intakes to the limit to see how much a horse can tolerate, and they have succeeded in feeding horses a third of their daily energy as oil – equivalent to 40 MJ or (1.5kg–3.3lb) per day.

❑ A 'glug', that typical way of adding oil to the feed, can weigh between 100g and 200g (3.5oz and 7oz), but for an effect on coat, less than 100g is needed.

❑ Choose your oil source according to what you want it to do: soya and linseed oils, and those found in grass, all supply linolenic acid, good for coat condition. All vegetable oils are equally good as providers of energy. Fish oils (but not fish-liver oils) and specific fatty acids called DHA and EPA are good for combating inflammation.

❑ When adding oil to the diet of competition horses, it is recommended that this begins at least six weeks before the competition season commences. The physiological significance of this is that it allows Type IIA muscle fibres to adapt to its use and to generate ATP aerobically (see Section 5, p.175).

Succulents commonly fed to horses

☐ Carrots
☐ Apples

Succulents less commonly fed to horses

☐ Parsnips
☐ Swedes
☐ Turnips
☐ Potatoes

Succulents

Something succulent will make the feed more appetizing and is another way of adding bulk. Fruits and vegetables are full of both water and sugar (or starch in the case of potatoes), and this is the essence of their succulence. They provide a taste of summer, and are usually fed as a treat to make a feed more exciting. Take care to remove any soil from root vegetables, as this can harbour disease. Nowadays, such succulents are fed in small amounts, but at one time carrots, swedes and mangolds were used in large quantities in heavy horse diets. Rates of 12.5–13.5kg (28–30lb) per day were not uncommon, and are still fed today by some heavy horse keepers. As a rough guide, 8kg (18lb) of carrots or apples is equivalent to 1kg (2.2lb) of barley or 1.3kg (3lb) of oats.

All succulents should be chopped longitudinally or left whole to avoid the risk of choking. Some owners combine the succulence of swedes and their size to make an alternative to expensive horse toys, by hanging one in the stable to keep the horse occupied.

Nutrient Supplements

Although technically described under feed legislation as 'complementary compound feeds', being mixtures of one or more feed ingredients and additives, nutrient supplements, combinations of varying vitamins and minerals, plus or minus the so-called nutraceuticals, fill many pots on feed store shelves. There are two broad categories within nutrient supplements:

Broad-spectrum: These contain, as their name suggests, a broad spectrum of major and trace minerals together with vitamins, and they are designed for topping up micronutrient levels where little or no hard feed is fed.

Specific: Specific supplements contain an ingredient or mixture of ingredients designed to perform a specific function, for instance, hoof supplements or electrolytes.

What is a nutraceutical?

These are defined as 'any non-toxic food component that has scientifically proven health benefits, including disease treatment or prevention', and as such are slightly different from classical nutrients. Nutraceuticals are nutrients credited with some pharmaceutical properties. Nutraceuticals are not drugs, however, and are not subject to the same legislative controls, which means they are often cheaper than drugs, but are not necessary as proven.

The most common nutraceuticals are those designed to support joints. Glucosamine appears to be the most effective joint supplement and has been shown both to be absorbed and taken up in articular cartilage. Chondroitin sulphate is also a frequent ingredient in joint formulations, as is MSM (methyl sulphonyl methane).

Herbs

Herbs occupy the middle ground between medicines and foods, and may be regarded as plant nutraceuticals. The term 'herb' describes a wide range of plants known to have properties ranging from therapeutic to nourishing. Like nutraceuticals, herbs are not subject to the same controls and trials for efficacy as drugs, but as 'ancient remedies', have, however, been proven down the ages.

The notion of horses in the recent past – before modern agricultural methods took hold – grazing large areas, naturally selecting herbs as they went, is probably flawed, and the author suspects you would have to go back many hundreds of years to find such Utopian pasture. Intensive farming has little to do with the lack of herbs. With the exception of stud pastures, equine pasture management has generally been badly neglected, so that even the most determined herbs would have found survival difficult.

Herbalists believe that the many compounds in herbs work together to produce their beneficial effect; in contrast, a pharmaceutical company would probably purify the ingredient considered most active. A good example is in pain-relievers: herbalism promotes willow fronds, whereas pharmacologists use the active ingredient, salicylic acid, the active component of aspirin.

Digestive Aids

An area of supplementation that has increased in popularity in recent years is that of digestive enhancement, or more correctly, digestive support. The terms and definitions that are used are complex and interrelated, and can lead to some confusion. For instance, any digestive aid is in fact acting as a probiotic, a term that literally means 'for life', and suggests active support of the digestive system. However, in practical feeding, the name probiotic is usually associated with one of a number of digestive aids – in fact, generally speaking there are three main categories of digestive aid available in most feed stores: yeasts, probiotics and prebiotics.

YEASTS Most of us are aware of yeast, basically minute fungi, used in brewing and bread making. However, they perform a different role within equine nutrition, working in the hindgut to stimulate microbial fermentation and so improve fibre digestion as a result. Yeasts *per se* are also a rich source of B vitamins (think about yeast-extract foods such as Marmite). The forms of yeast available in horse feeds are live yeasts (usually *Saccharomyces cerevisiae 1026*), dead yeasts and brewers' yeasts. It is thought that only live yeasts exhibit the hindgut fermentation-altering characteristics described above, although there is little

Use of digestive enhancers

The use of all such digestive enhancers, and indeed many feed additives generally, is governed by EU legislation. Currently very few of the additives used in horse feeds and supplements are authorized, a process that requires a proof of safety and effectiveness of the particular additive through research trials. The dearth of a body of research currently on such supplements suggests that some types use may be limited by legislation in the future.

research to compare the efficacy of the varying forms.

PROBIOTICS Products marketed as probiotics are usually preparations of bacterial cultures designed to encourage a good balance of intestinal microflora in the small intestine. (Whilst we tend to think that microbes only exist in the hindgut, this is not the case and there is also significant microbial presence in the small intestine.)

The mode of action of such probiotic preparations has not been closely studied in horses; however, it is thought that their addition promotes 'healthy' bacteria populations and excludes pathogenic (disease-causing) bacteria. They may also generate additional digestive enzymes to assist in the breakdown of food.

A key feature of probiotics is the number and type of bacteria that are contained in them. Look for cultures that provide 10^8 or 10^9 organisms per gram, and contain species that are able to withstand the high acidity of the stomach and the conditions in the small intestine. Otherwise a probiotic will be nothing more than an expensive protein supplement.

PREBIOTICS This term covers non-microbial feed additives that stimulate microbial growth in the digestive system of the horse, and are usually derived from complex carbohydrate sources.

Mannan-oligosaccharides (MOS) are indigestible complex sugars found in yeast cell walls that are thought to bind to pathogenic bacteria in the small intestine, and so remove them. Constant control against pathogenic bacterial populations in the small intestine contributes a significant proportion of the daily work of the horse's immune-system load, particularly in young animals, therefore removing them is thought to allow the immune system to function more effectively. However, there is very little scientific work to substantiate this theory.

Fructo-oligosaccharides (FOS) are also prebiotics, but these are composed of a different group of complex sugars. These are thought to work by providing the appropriate energy source for beneficial bacteria to grow in the small and large intestines, so promote a healthy gut environment.

Treats

These are, as their name suggests, small hand-held offerings, fed in small amounts to reward a horse or pony. There has been a huge growth in the numbers of treats available, all challenging the supremacy of the Polo mint (in the UK) as the reward of choice.

2 Science into Practice: Feeding Principles

In this section

❑ The rules of good feeding   55
  Temperament and condition
  Guidelines for horse weights
  Guidelines for work levels

❑ Calculating the basic ration   60

❑ Feeding for a contented horse   62

❑ Feed management   64
  When to feed

❑ Poisonous plants   66

❑ Types of feed   68
  Understanding a feed label
  Prohibited substances

❑ Choosing a product   74

Making the choice

The most common cry on feed company helplines is this: 'There are so many products to choose from, I don't know what to feed.' Not only is there a huge number of fed products, there's a wide variety of advice out there too, from friends, riding instructors, college lecturers, veterinarians and nutritionists. However, not all of them give the same, or even correct advice on any particular issue.

Before you 'phone a friend', do your homework in this section. Successful feeding is all about knowing your horse, obeying the rules of good feeding, and following some basic guidelines.

THE RULES OF GOOD FEEDING

These need no introduction, having been honed throughout centuries of feeding. Nowadays we may know more about the science behind them, but they work as well as we know they did before the Industrial Revolution. While they are all important, they are listed below in order of the thought process you should go through when feeding:

1 Allow access to fresh, clean water at all times.

2 Feed according to the temperament and condition of the horse.

3 Feed according to the bodyweight of the horse.

4 Feed for work done, not in anticipation of the work the horse is about to do.

5 Feed plenty of fibre for healthy gut function. Aim for a minimum of 50 per cent of the diet as roughage.

6 Feed by weight, not volume of feed: weigh a scoop and a typical haynet.

7 Feed at the same time each day. Horses are creatures of habit and like a settled routine.

8 Feed little and often to mimic the horse's digestive physiology. Keep feeds of concentrates to 2–2.5kg(4–5lb) per feed.

9 Use high quality feeds. Do not feed dusty or mouldy feed.

10 Make any changes to the diet gradually so as to reduce the risk of digestive upset.

11 Don't exercise immediately after feeding: allow two to three hours after feeding before working the horse and do not feed until one hour after working.

Temperament and Condition

These are the great deciders of how much and what to feed, as each horse interacts differently with its feed. Very excitable horses may not be big eaters, and so it may be difficult to persuade them to eat as much as you would wish, and these horses may have difficulty in maintaining their weight. The following table provides some rules of thumb as to how much to feed.

Overweight/ native ponies	1.55–1.75% of bodyweight
Good doers (easy keepers)/horses in light-medium work	2% of bodyweight
Lactating mares/ poor doers (difficult keepers)/in hard work	2.5% of bodyweight

A lactating mare requires extra energy to ensure a health supply of milk for the foal

Guidelines for Horse Weights

Knowing the horse's weight is essential for accurate feed planning, and also for the administration of correct doses of both medicines and wormers.

A horse's weight can be measured in a variety of ways, the most common being on a weighbridge (weight scale), or by using a weigh tape. A weighbridge is the most accurate, especially if you want to monitor weight change regularly, but weigh tapes are a good alternative for checking how much a horse weighs from time to time. There are also a variety of equations that can be used to calculate weight, involving measurements of girth, body length and so on.

The table below gives typical weights for a variety of horse types and breeds:

Using a weigh tape

Breed	Approx. height (hh)	Girth (cm)	Bodyweight guide in kg (lb)
Dartmoor pony	11	140	200–250 (440–550)
Welsh pony Section A & B	12	145	250–350 (550–771)
Riding pony	13	155	350–450 (771–991)
Welsh Section C	13.2	160	300–400 (661–881)
New Forest	14	165	350–450 (771–991)
Arab	14	170	400–450 (881–991)
Welsh Cob/Fell	14.2	175	450–500 (991–1,102)
Small hunter	15	180	475–520 (1,047–1,146)
Riding horse	15.2	185	500–550 (1,102–1,210)
Thoroughbred	16	190	500–550 (1,102–1,210)
Irish sport horse	16.2	195	550–600 (1,212–1,323)
Warmblood	17	205	580–640 (1,279–1,411)
Shire	18	210	700–800 (1,540–1763)

Guidelines for Work Levels

As with our own diets, it is easy to overestimate the work done or energy used at a particular exercise level. It is therefore equally possible to overfeed in relation to the work done.

The following table is a guide to categorizing the daily activities of horses into the common denominations of maintenance, light, medium, and hard work. The horse has an enormous capacity for work over and above levels that humans would consider strenuous for themselves. As a consequence, most leisure horses in the UK are truly at maintenance or in light work, and most competition horses can be classified as in medium work. The following table provides a guide:

Level of work	Typical activity
Maintenance	Horses and ponies not working (at rest)
Light work	Hacking: leisure riding (approx. 1–2 hours a day)
	Show horses: local shows, novice level
	Dressage: prelim/novice standard
	Show jumping: local shows, BSJA British Novice, Discovery
	Racehorses: early fittening work
	Endurance: 20-mile (30km) rides at slow pace
	Novice level eventing (unaffiliated)
	Police horses
Medium work	Showing: affiliated, show circuit showing
	Dressage: BD medium, advanced medium
	Show jumpers: BSJA Newcomers, Foxhunters
	Eventing: BE intermediate and advanced one-day events
	Endurance: 50-mile (80km) rides
	Showjumping: BSJA opens for grades B & A horses
	Racing: fast canter work
Hard work	Hunting: two full days per week
	Dressage: BD grand prix
	Eventing: BE 3- and 4-star three-day events
	Endurance: race rides
	Racehorses in full training and racing

Be careful in your assessment of the horse's true workload and feed according to the work done

Calculating the Basic Ration

How much and what to feed? The choice is endless, but here's a quick guide:

Level of work	Forage % of diet	Hard feed % of diet	Typical hard feed type
Maintenance	80–100	0–20	Low energy
Light work	70–100	0–30	Low energy
Medium work	40–60	40–60	Low or medium energy
Hard work	30–50	50–70	Medium or high energy
In-foal mare, last 3 months	40–60	40–60	Medium or high energy
Mare lactating	40–60	40–60	High energy

Although we're always encouraged to weigh out feeds, most of us still talk in scoops and slices. The following is a guide to typical amounts:

Feedstuff	Typical weight
Slice of hay	2kg (4lb)
Large haynet	8kg (18lb)
Bale of hay	20kg (44lb)
Small bale of haylage	25kg (56lb)
Large bale of haylage	200kg (440lb)
Standard scoop of cubes	1.5kg (3lb)
Standard scoop of mix (sweet feed)	1kg (2lb)
Double handful of chop or chaff	250g (8–9oz)
Standard bucket of chop or chaff	1kg (2lb 3oz)
Typical glug of oil	100g (3–4oz)

Finally, check the health status of the horse or pony in your care: laminitis-risk cases, those that suffer from respiratory allergy, are prone to colic or tying up, or that suffer from any other diet-related ailments, will require special consideration over and above the rules of thumb given above. Guidance on these special cases is given in Section 4.

It is clear that the appetite levels and energy and protein requirements for horses and ponies of varying weight will also vary.

Feed intakes should be based on 2 per cent of their bodyweight for horses at maintenance, and in light or medium work. It should be based on 2.5 per cent of bodyweight for those in hard work. These figures are a guide only, and will have to be adjusted according to the individual horse.

You can use this information to calculate your own horse's daily diet.

For example:

Your horse	A 15.2hh riding horse, in good condition and of even temperament, that holds its weight well. Estimated weight 525kg (1,158lb)
Workload	You ride out on most days for about an hour, school once a week, and go to local shows or riding club events at weekends. Light work
	Guide to total amount of feed per day: 525kg x 2% = 10.5kg (23lb) of feed per day.
Forage	70–100% of total feed = 7.4–10.5kg (16–23lb), equivalent to 4–5 slices of hay, or just under half a bale per day.
Hard feed	0–30% of total feed = between 0–3kg (0–7lb), the maximum is equivalent to just over two scoops of low energy cubes or three scoops of low energy mix (sweet feed). (If no hard feed is offered, then a broad spectrum or general purpose supplement is advised to provide the necessary micronutrients that may be deficient in the forage. See 'Supplements' p.46.)

Feeding for a Contented Horse

As the rule of good feeding says, horses are creatures of habit, and seem happier when a constant day-to-day routine is followed. Feeding at the same time each day contributes to a happier horse – but food is more important to a horse than that, because within every stabled horse is a free roamer at heart. For a really happy horse it is essential to allow him a lifestyle as near to a field-kept horse as possible, and fitting this around the lifestyle of many horse owners who go out to work can create a unique set of challenges.

If you work, your horse has a long day ahead once you've tended to him in the morning until you return in the evening. This applies especially in the winter, or if the horse is stabled at any time of year. Both are situations when the horse is totally reliant on you for its daily food.

Keeping Horses Happy

Feed forage on an *ad libitum* basis
If this is not possible, feed several small forage meals throughout the day, or use other sources of fibre such as low energy forage replacers.

Feed forage on the floor
This encourages natural feeding behaviour, it maintains correct jaw action and so minimizes tooth wear, and it also allows for airway drainage.

Feed horses individually
Feed horses on their own, or if they must feed in a group, ensure that each gets his allowance.

Remove bullies from groups when feeding.

Give hard feed three or four times per day if possible.

If not turned out, allow within both sight and sound of other horses.

Increase exercise or turnout times.

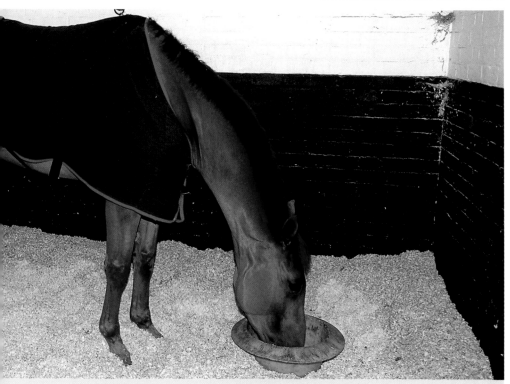

Where possible feed from the floor as this allows the correct jaw action that minimizes tooth wear

Food for thought: eating time facts

- ❑ Horses in the wild spend 66 per cent of their time eating, equivalent to about sixteen hours per day.
- ❑ Stabled or field-kept horses and ponies with free access to forage also 'graze' for this length of time.
- ❑ It takes a horse about 20min to eat 1kg (2.2lb) of hay; thus an average 5kg (11lb) haynet will last 1hr 40mins.
- ❑ Compound feeds take about 8min to eat per kg (2.2lb).

This is all well and good if forage is offered on an *ad libitum* basis, but often it happens that it is restricted, either because the horse eats up while you're out, or because you deliberately restrict him because he is a good doer (easy keeper), to prevent unwanted excessive weight gain. However, a decrease in eating time significantly increases the time he is not feeding, and this is when he is at high risk of developing stereotypies (see Section 4).

Feed Management

The feed room, or area where the feed is kept, must contain secure, rodent-proof containers for good storage. In addition it must be cool and out of direct sunlight, as heat will dry out the feed and can reduce the potency of any vitamins and minerals present, especially if a bag is open for some time. It goes without saying that feed should be kept in a dry area, as water ingress will rapidly spoil it.

The feed room, buckets, mangers, feed scoops and water drinkers must be kept scrupulously clean, to prevent the build-up of mould and general dirt, and, especially with spilled feed, to prevent attracting vermin. The characteristically musty smell in some feed rooms is likely to be that of a chronic infestation of grain mite, those minute pests whose eggs lie dormant in most feed cereals, and wait for conditions of warmth and moisture in order to hatch. Once they are hatched, dirty utensils will spread the infestation into new feeds.

Keep the feed room tidy to avoid encouraging vermin

Feed room equipment

The following is a list of all the equipment ideally kept in, or close to, the feed room:

❏ Storage containers

❏ Scoops

❏ Mixing spoon or paddle

❏ Spring balance for checking weights of feed

❏ Shelves for small pack items

❏ Sink and washing equipment

❏ Tap and running water

❏ Power point and kettle

❏ Brush or vacuum cleaner for clearing up spilt feed (clearly a vacuum cleaner will be ineffective if hay and feeds are stored together)

How long will a bag or bale last?

Feedstuff	Feed rate	Days
Bale of hay	8kg (18lb)/day (4 slices)	2.5
20kg (44lb) sack of cubes	1.5kg (3lb)/day (1 standard scoop)	13
	3kg (7lb)/day (2 scoops)	6
	6kg (13lb) /day (2 scoops)	3
20kg (44lb) sack of mix	1kg (2lb)/day (1 standard scoop)	20
	2kg (4lb)/day (2 scoops)	10
	4kg (9lb)/day (4 scoops)	5
20kg (44lb) sack of feed balancer	500g (1lb)/day	40
20kg (44lb) sack of chaff	500g/day	40

When to Feed

The precise timing of feeds, particularly in relation to high performance horses, is often tricky. Plenty of science is emerging, but not so that concrete feed guidelines can be laid down. We do know that the following parameters should be observed in the best interests of the horse, and for optimum performance:

- Little and often feeding systems work, as there are no peaks and troughs in nutrient flow, and no major shifts in fluid balance throughout the day.
- Forage binds water as it passes through the digestive system, and this is both a help and a hindrance. It helps, because the water acts as a fluid and electrolyte reservoir; and it hinders because that water is equivalent to extra weight, which in some cases is a disadvantage. Feeding large amounts of forage to a racehorse will slow it up, whereas optimizing forage intakes in, say, endurance horses is an advantage.
- Large, single meals divert blood to the intestine for approximately two hours after a meal.
- Following a feed it then takes about two hours for the food to appear as nutrients in the bloodstream. Insulin is stimulated to remove any blood sugar to the tissues, and this can take up to five hours. Exercising within this time may mean that tissue energy sources are below optimum.

Rules of Thumb

- Wait for at least one hour after feeding before imposing even gentle exercise on the horse.
- For intense work, wait for 4–5 hours after feeding, and if competing early in the morning, the last hard feed should be the night before.

Poisonous Plants

Almost anything, including water, is poisonous if fed in extreme proportions. However, there are certain plants that are poisonous to horses if they are ingested. Worldwide the list of plants that can affect a horse is immense, so here we concentrate on those a horse is most likely to come into contact with.

A poisonous plant is defined as one that, when eaten, causes a departure from normal health. Most animals, including horses and ponies, do not normally graze poisonous plants, but this is not a guarantee that poisoning will never take place. Rarely is a horse poisoned by just a single mouthful, however (except in the case of hemlock and yew); most poisonings take place after a significant intake has occurred, usually over a period of weeks or from season to season.

The following are occasions when a horse may consume a poisonous plant:

- ❑ If it is dried within forage, particularly ragwort.
- ❑ In overgrazed fields when grass is insignificant, and poisonous plants are amongst the only plants available.
- ❑ During times of extreme drought when other vegetation is severely limited.
- ❑ On first turn-out, especially amongst youngstock.

Poisoning can take many forms in a horse, from producing blisters and excess production of saliva, to those that cause digestive upset, photosensitization, liver disease, neurological problems, anaemia or sudden death. In the UK, by far the most common form of poisoning is that from the ingestion of ragwort (see Section 4). However, it is good advice to become familiar with what other poisonous plants look like.

The table below gives a guide to the more common poisonous plants, how they act, their source, and the likely incidence of poisoning.

Ragwort: a common cause of poisoning

Common poisonous plants

Plant	Effect	Source	Likelihood
Ragwort	Liver damage	Grazing ragwort-infested land; or hay that is made from contaminated grazing	Common
Buttercup	Excess salivation, colic, diarrhoea	Infested grazing; (not poisonous when dried)	Uncommon, despite large numbers of buttercups found in horse grazing.
Green oak leaves, green acorns	Hard faeces followed by diarrhoea	Oak trees in grazing or overhanging pasture	Uncommon, most horses likely to ingest when leaves and acorns on the ground and therefore past the green stage.
Foxglove	Diarrhoea, rapid death	Hedgerows	Uncommon
St John's Wort	Photosensitization	Excessive supplementation	Rare
Horse or mare's tail	Reluctance to move, digestive upset	In grazing, or hay made from contaminated grazing	Rare
Bracken	Reluctance to move Roaring	In grazing, especially in heath or moorland areas	Rare
Black walnut	Oedema, colic	Wood shavings made from the wood	Rare
Hemlock (European) or water hemlock	Salivation, muscle tremors, paralysis, death	Hedgerows, pond areas	Rare
Yew	Rapid death	Churchyards, gardens, hedges	Rare

Types of Feed

Below is a brief guide to the nutrient specifications of the various compound feed types on the market today.

Nutrient specifications						
Feed type	Typical name	Energy content (MJ/d)	Protein	Oil	Fibre	Vitamins and minerals
Maintenance	High fibre, basic economy	9–10	8–10	2–3	16–22	Low
Light work	Horse and pony, cool, working	9–11	10–11	2–4	10–16	Medium
Competition	Competition, sports	10–12	10–13	2–6	7–15	Medium
Intense work	Racing, stamina	11–13	12–14	4–10	5–12	High
Breeding	Stud, grower, developer	11–13	14–16	3–6	5–13	High

Remember to increase the ration as you step up the intensity of your training programme

Understanding a Feed Label

The packaging of all manufactured feeds and supplements must contain by law certain information that describes their purpose and nutritional content. This information is contained within what is known as the statutory statement, and the content is set down by government law, which in Europe is in turn dictated by European law.

The statutory statement is similar, but not the same as the labelling on human foods. A typical label is shown below:

Individual bag number   **Formulation reference**
#SSSSSSS   0142/6061

THE HORSE FEEDS COMPANY
The Feed Mill, Country Lane, Anytown AA1 2BB

Statutory Statement
Net weight given on bag or delivery order. Store in cool dry conditions.
800 HORSE & PONY CUBES
A complementary feedstuff for feeding to equines in conjunction with forage
at a rate of up to 8kg per horse per day.

Oil 3.00% Protein 10.50% Fibre 15.00% Ash 10.30%

Ingredient declaration
INGREDIENTS:
Wheatfeed, oatfeed, barley, soya, molasses, minerals and vitamins

Best before date
Best before (Vitamins guaranteed present until) end of 01-DEC-03

Vitamin A	(iu/kg)	10,000
Vitamin D3	(iu/kg)	1,500
Vitamin E – alpha tocopherol	(iu/kg)	37
Selenium – sodium selenite	(mg/kg)	0.2
Copper – cupric sulphate	(mg/kg)	22

Contains butylated hydroxyanisole (BHA)

Establishment number
GB 870 0015 (establishment's number)

Guide to the Content of the Label

Individual bag number and formulation reference code

Although not strictly required on the statutory statement, good manufacturing practice dictates that in the event of a query, any part of the product can be traced right back to the individual production run. If, for instance, a complaint is ever made against a product, the company will use this information to investigate how, and if, the issue arose within the manufacturing process.

Statutory statement

Required by law. This must indicate the purpose for which the feed is intended, and must state the oil, crude protein, crude fibre and ash content, expressed as percentages. In addition to this, the vitamin A, D and E content must be declared, along with the total content of the trace elements selenium, and copper, if a supplement containing these has been added. Other nutrients can be stated if a company wishes to do so, but these are mandatory. Energy, however, may not be stated within the statutory statement, and this is because there is no one agreed prediction equation for the energy content of feeds. (See also p.145 Section 5, 'Nutrients and their Digestion'.)

Ingredients

These must be listed by ingredient in descending order, according to wording decreed in the legislation.

'Best before' date

It is required by law that 'Vitamins present until' be stated. This gives the horse owner an indication of the shelf life of the product. Most horse feeds carry between three and six months' shelf life, and supplements six months to one year.

Antioxidants

There is a distinction between nutrient antioxidants that operate at tissue level, and those added during the manufacturing process to prevent feed spoilage. There is a defined list of those used, and their use must be acknowledged in the statutory statement. (See also p.168 Section 5, 'Antioxidants'.)

Establishment's number

In the aftermath of BSE, the requirement for complete traceability throughout the food chain means that every manufacturer must be authorized to make animal feeds. The 'establishment's number' identifies that this is so.

Weight:

At some point on the packaging, the product must state the weight of the goods. If not printed elsewhere on the tub or bag, it must be stated within the statutory statement.

In horse feed manufacture, some companies print the statutory statement on their bags, whilst others stitch it into the top of the bag. For the most part, supplements have the information printed on the packaging.

Prohibited Substances

Many horse feeds and supplements carry a form of words stating either their suitability 'for feeding to horses competing under Jockey Club or FEI rules', or that they are free from both caffeine and theobromine. The principle behind the rules regarding prohibited substances is that all competition should be won or lost on the merits of the horse and rider, and not enhanced by unfair means.

A 'prohibited substance' as defined by the Jockey Club and FEI is one originating externally to the horse, whether or not it is natural (endogenous) to the horse, and which falls within any of the categories contained in a defined list. For the most part we think of drugs in relation to illegal performance enhancement, but under the terms of the list, feeds do not escape having the potential to cause a dope test failure.

As science advances at speed, the list of prohibited substances produced by the Jockey Club and FEI is unspecific, and stipulates 'substances acting on the nervous system, those acting on the cardiovascular system, the respiratory system, urinary, reproductive, blood and immune systems, and the digestive and musculo-skeletal systems', rather than chemical or brand names.

In addition to the generic list, there is also a list of other substances that occur naturally in the horse or its feedstuffs, to which a zero-tolerance approach in blood or urine samples would be impractical. These include hydrocortisone and testosterone, and from feed, theobromine, salicylic acid and the heavy metal arsenic. Herbs such as valerian are also not permitted.

The biggest risk of feed contamination comes from theobromine, a metabolite of caffeine found in biscuit and coffee residues. Most manufacturers operate strict 'no caffeine' policies that range from supplier and haulier agreements not to handle caffeine-containing materials, to no-caffeine buying policies, together with positive release, so that no product is sold until the results of a caffeine and theobromine test have tested negative.

Another potential feed contaminant is morphine; opium poppies are most likely to be the source of morphine in feeds, and they grow in certain climatic areas of Europe. The risk of contamination is reduced by not sourcing cereals or cereal products from these areas.

Herbal products exist in a grey area, as in many cases their use goes undetected, even though they are often fed because of their therapeutic benefits. Valerian, a herb with calmative properties, is one herb that is tested for, and for complete safety it is wise to consult the company marketing a herbal product as to its status in this respect before use.

If you intend your horse to race check with the feed company that the products you use don't contain substances prohibited by any governing bodies

Choosing a Product

All feed companies are not equal. Some manufacture their products themselves, others, like Marks and Spencers, have their products made for them; some employ nutritionists and technical staff, others use consultants; and some are accredited by quality assurance, such as ISO9002, others are not. None of this may be immediately apparent in the feed retailer when making your choice; indeed, all the horse owner requires is a feed that will work for their horse. Nevertheless, with the large variety of products available, choosing can be daunting. For the most part, we don't tend to change the feed unless a problem arises, but when a new diet is required, apply the following checklist of criteria when choosing:

❑ Read up, ask an expert, or talk to a company Helpline about the feed decision and the reason behind it.

❑ Choose the product type that sounds most suitable (eg low energy feed).

❑ Check out the claims made for those available in local feed stores, and if necessary, telephone the company for further information. Some claims made sound too good to be true, and it may be worth a quick call to check that the claim is justified; look for research results, or field trials using horses of a similar kind to the one you are enquiring about.

❑ Ask what quality accreditations the company holds for the manufacture of feeds: if you think about it, we handle horse feed far more than other pet or even animal feeds, and it's worth a double check that quality procedures are in place to avoid contamination such as salmonella.

In terms of horse-feed quality assurance there are currently two well known systems: ISO9002, an International Standard of quality assurance practices in manufacturing, and the UKASTA Feed Assurance Scheme, which checks manufacturers against a high-level quality checklist of good manufacturing practice and ingredient sourcing, specifically designed to maximize food safety, and endorsed by all the main UK grocery chains.

Calling a feed helpline

Information to have at hand when calling a feed company helpline:

❑ Horse details: Name, height, estimated weight, condition, temperament.

❑ Description of the work, stage of growth, stage of pregnancy, lactation etc.

❑ The weight (failing that, the number of slices and scoops) of feed, forage and supplements used, and the brand names used.

❑ Description of the grazing available, how many acres, how many horses etc.

❑ Description of recent feeding history (changes in grazing, forage, feeds used, workload and so on, and any comments from the horse's veterinary surgeon that may apply).

Always remember to measure feed accurately: don't guess

3 Problem Solver:

Feeding to Requirement

In this section

❏ The horse feed year   78

❏ Feeding your first horse or pony   80

❏ Feeding the pony   82

❏ Feeding the excitable horse   84

❏ Feeding the competition horse   86

❏ Feeding the older horse or pony   90

❏ Feeding the brood mare   92

❏ Feeding the stallion   96

❏ Feeding youngstock   98

❏ Feeding the orphaned foal   100

❏ Feeding the racehorse   102

❏ Feeding box-resting horses   104

❏ Feeding to put condition on a horse   106

❏ Feeding to lose weight   110

The Horse Feed Year

From time to time everyone has a feeding query unique to their horse and their situation. Many queries have the same issues at their core however, and this whole section is devoted to the most frequently asked questions related to feeding horses. Below are the 'top ten', and you will find the answers to these and many others in the following pages, or in the following section on diet-related ailments.

As the saying goes, prevention is always better than cure, and there are certain times of the year when sitting down and giving a little thought and consideration about what to feed may avoid problems related to feeding later on. The table opposite will serve as a handy reminder.

'TOP TEN' FEEDING QUERIES

1   'I have just purchased a new horse and I would like to check that I am feeding him correctly.'

2   'My mare is very excitable, and keeps spooking at imaginary horrors around every corner. Could the feed be making her like this?'

3   'I have noticed that my daughter's pony has lost a lot of weight through the winter. What should I feed him to put the weight back on?'

4   'The vet has just diagnosed laminitis in our Welsh pony; what sort of diet should I feed him?'

5   'I have an overweight Irish Draught mare. Can you help me draw up a diet for her?'

6   'My horse has just had an attack of azoturia so I need to review what I feed.'

7   'I am thinking of buying a two-year-old, and would like some advice on how to feed it before I make the purchase.'

8   'My gelding is twenty-three years old: should he be on a veteran mix?'

9   'I want to build up my horse's topline. Which feed should I use?'

10   'My pony can't manage hay because he has very poor teeth: what can I do?'

DO'S

SPRING (MRCH–APRIL/MAY)

- ❑ Decide what to feed for the active season ahead.
- ❑ If your horse will be stabled, make sure you have a good supply of consistent forage to see you through to the end of the year. Get it analysed if competing.
- ❑ Choose hard feeds plus added extras (supplements, etc) according to workload. Consult a nutritionist or company helpline.

DON'TS

- ❑ In early season work, don't increase the level of work too sharply; this will show up in below par performance, a dull coat, or in a poor blood test (see Section 4).
- ❑ Don't cut the forage back too far as the hard feed increases; horses will tend to limit themselves as the workload increases.
- ❑ Don't allow ponies/horses prone to laminitis too much spring grass.

SUMMER (MAY/JUNE–AUGUST)

- ❑ Watch out for changes in temperament, condition etc, and adjust feed accordingly.
- ❑ Monitor the quality of your grazing.
- ❑ Have a mid-season review to check that all is well.
- ❑ In late June/July/early August: choose winter forage, look for good quality, and have an analysis done.

- ❑ Don't forget electrolytes when working and travelling, (see p.164).
- ❑ Don't automatically blame the feed when things go wrong. Check out other factors, such as a change in management, even if only for one day, which may have caused an upset.

AUTUMN (SEPTEMBER–OCTOBER)

- ❑ Look out for an autumn flush of grass growth that may cause laminitis or a change in behaviour.
- ❑ Grass growth slows down and its nutritional worth deteriorates from October – add extra hay to the diet.

- ❑ Don't make sudden changes to the diet, such as adding large amounts of a conditioning feed all at once to the rations of a horse that has lost condition.
- ❑ Don't feed poor quality forages.

WINTER (NOVEMBER–FEBRUARY)

- ❑ Do remember haylage is 40% water, and therefore a greater volume needs to be fed to supply the same weight of nutrients as hay.
- ❑ Feed according to work done.

- ❑ Don't limit haylage intakes.
- ❑ Don't forget electrolytes when working or travelling (see p.164).
- ❑ Don't forget micronutrient intakes in horses not in work (see p.162).

Feeding Your First Horse or Pony

At last the ramp comes down, and out steps the new equine person in your life – but don't leave it until this moment to consider how to look after him. Feeding him is a very important part of his care, and, given how much horses like their food, this is one of the best ways to 'bond' with him.

The checklist opposite is a simplified version of the rules of good feeding (see Section 2, p.55) that should run through your mind when selecting the appropriate feeds for your (first) horse.

Feeding Tactics

First, find our what the horse was fed at his previous home
- ❏ Ask the make and the type, the amounts offered, and if there is any particular reason why that feed was used.

Be prepared
- ❏ Make sure you have some hay and feed for your new charge, when he arrives at his new home.

Remember the rules
- ❏ Keep the rules of good feeding uppermost in your mind (see Section 2, p.55).

Don't kill him with kindness
- ❏ Feed at maintenance or light work levels until you have got to know the horse. Whilst it may be very tempting to lovingly feed scoopfuls of mix to your new friend, his behaviour will almost certainly be better if hard feeds are used with manufacturers' guidelines.

Try the fail-safe diet
- ❏ Start with a diet of 80–100 per cent forage, and 0–20 per cent of a low energy, high fibre hard feed, preferably a cube or pellet (the amounts will depend on the condition of the horse). This is a fail-safe diet that will not precipitate either diet-related ailments or misbehaviour.

Keep it simple
- ❏ Don't overcomplicate your feeding regime, and if in doubt, phone one or more of the feed company helplines.

Checklist

What work are you going to do?
Whether it is a first pony for a child, a hack for an adult, or a retired racehorse, your chosen activity will affect the amount and type of feed the horse will need.

Stabled, at grass, at home, or at livery?
Keeping a horse outside in winter means he will need more supplementary food to help him keep himself warm and to prevent him losing weight. In spring and summer, when the grass grows, you will require less supplementary feed, as the horse will put on weight. Keeping him at livery also usually means a finite area for feed storage and restricted grazing.

What is his temperament like, and how does he hold his weight and body condition?
How a horse is bred will often dictate temperament, which in turn affects whether a horse loses or gains weight easily.

Age and tooth quality
A first horse or pony, especially a 'schoolmaster', may be a bit 'long in the tooth', and the state of his teeth will dictate the type of feed you should use. Also, make sure his teeth are rasped/ checked by a vet or an equine dental technician.

Does he suffer from any specific diet-related issues?
For instance, allergies to dust, laminitis etc (see Section4).

Get educated
Feed company helplines can provide good feed management advice, as well as product recommendations. Riding clubs and the Pony Club both offer training schemes for improving stable management skills.

Feeding the Pony

Ponies come in all shapes and sizes, and are usually either pure-bred native (in the UK there are twelve breeds), or they are part native and part either Thoroughbred or Arab. However, their 'native genes' exert a strong influence in the way they interact with their food. Native ponies evolved to live off poor quality grazing of variable supply, and consequently are expert at maintaining themselves on low energy, high fibre feeds. The variation between the feast of spring and the famine of winter means they are 'pre-programmed' to convert food to fat in spring and summer, storing it for use in the winter months when historically food was not available.

Spring/Summer

During spring and summer, ponies' exercise levels increase because there are many more opportunities for their owners to ride, at shows, competitions and Pony Club activities. At the same time the grass is growing rapidly, and even the most horse-sick pasture is capable of over-providing energy and protein at this time. As ponies tend to be more prone to laminitis than horses, managing their access to grazing is important: turning ponies out on lush grass is not advisable, and a bare paddock should be made available for overweight ponies. (See 'Feeding to lose weight', and 'Feeding the older horse' in this chapter, and Section 4, common nutrition-related diseases: 'Laminitis', p.118.)

Autumn/Winter

During the winter, native ponies should be tough enough to winter out; however, ponies with Thoroughbred blood may not be. Field shelters or high hedges should protect out-wintered ponies from the worst weather. Good quality hay should be fed at regular intervals (every day), and if necessary the pony should be rugged.

Feeding Tactics

Feed grass and hay

❑ Grass and hay can sustain the energy and protein requirements of a pony at maintenance or in light work, such as hacking out, but not necessarily all the minerals.

Raise energy levels for increased activity

❑ For ponies undertaking regular Pony Club-type activities, energy requirements will be raised and a low energy, high fibre feed will provide sufficient energy without promoting misbehaviour or excess weight gain (cubes are lower in starch and sugar than mixes).

Typical feeding levels should be between 1–3kg (2–6lb) a day.

For ponies in very hard work, for example in regular competition, driving trials or hunting, a medium energy or competition feed can be given. Again, typical feeding levels are between 1–3kg a day.

Use chaff to control feed consumption

❑ Many ponies are greedy, and adding a chaff slows the rate of consumption, and is a good way to add bulk to a meagre ration. Double handfuls weigh between 0.5–1kg (1–2lb) a day.

Keep it simple

❑ For ponies with RAD (or COPD) or even a mild dust allergy (see p.138, Section 4 'Allergies and Intolerances'), or in times of a hay shortage, a complete fibre feed is a good alternative to hay. Again, these can be in the form of cubes or a chaff that contains added vitamins and minerals (see pp.34 and 42). These can be fed either as the whole or as part of the forage component of the diet.

Nutrient Focus

Dietary vitamin and mineral levels

Use a broad spectrum supplement if feeding an all-forage diet (see p.46, Section 1 'Supplements'), or less than the manufacturers' recommended level of compound feed.

Dietary energy supply

Ponies don't need too much energy. Pay particular attention to keeping the energy supply low in spring and early summer, and again in the early autumn when grass is growing quickly.

Feeding the Excitable Horse

For some horses, life seems just too good, and they approach most things in high spirits. Invariably this means riding out a horse that constantly jig-jogs or spooks at imaginary horrors in walls and hedges; others are more mischievous and may buck or rear when ridden. Whilst a horse's temperament is unique to itself, there is no doubt that the wrong kind of feed can affect the way it behaves.

Feeding Tactics

If feed is one of the contributing factors to excitability. There are three main areas to consider.

1 The amount being fed

❑ Is the horse receiving too much feed (see Section 2, 'Practical Feeding')? It may be that cutting the feed right down will moderate the horse's excitability.

2 The type of feed offered

❑ See p.148, Section 5 'Sources of Energy'

3 Calming supplements

❑ Few of these are proven scientifically, but old wives' tales and anecdotal reports suggest that some herbs (such as valerian and St John's Wort – see p.50) and megadoses of certain nutrients, are effective in calming excitable horses.

Nutrient Focus

With an excitable horse it is important to observe the following parameters when working out his diet:

Sources of energy
Keep fibre levels high and starch levels low (see also p.154).

Minerals and vitamins
If hard feed levels are kept to a minimum in horses that are excitable, then additional micronutrients will be required via a supplement (see p.162).

Nutrient megadoses
Magnesium, vitamin E and tryptophan (an amino acid that is an active factor in the hot milky drinks that send us to sleep at bedtime) have all been quoted at one time or another as being effective as calmatives for horses.

Health check

As well as considering the feeding of an excitable horse, the following health check will rule out any non-nutritional causes of excitable behaviour:

- ❑ **Poorly fitting tack or rugs:** seek advice from a saddler.
- ❑ Pain in the mouth from **teeth problems or a poorly fitting bit**: call in the equine dental technician.
- ❑ **Pain elsewhere, such as the back:** seek advice from a vet or physiotherapist.
- ❑ **Poor eyesight:** again, have a veterinary assessment.

Feeding the Competition Horse

Whilst the variety of equestrian sport continues to increase, and the level to which every individual aspires varies, the bottom line of feeding the competition horse is that he is fit enough to cope with the required intensity of work, and that the rider also has the necessary control and obedience, and power and stamina underneath him, at the appropriate time.

The factors that affect a horse's performance are so many and varied that feed is not always considered critical – though when a horse receives up to 12kg (26lb) a day of total feed, this cannot go without having some impact. It is easy to feed for power or stamina and lose control and obedience. Feeding according to temperament is probably one of the two most important rules of feeding competition horses (the first being to ensure there is a supply of clean fresh water available): the horse's temperament governs his willingness to obey and his ability to cope with the demands of competition. Otherwise, following the textbook rules of feeding horses according to work done is likely to lead to some exciting, if not controlled, performances.

All competition horses have to be fit to undertake their work, but the level of fitness required depends on the sport and the level of competition to which you aspire. Thus endurance horses, driving horses and event horses all require high levels of fitness, particularly that for stamina; dressage and show jumpers require a different kind of fitness, that of power generation; whilst for show horses a lesser level is sufficient.

Fit horses adapt so they generate energy principally by aerobic respiration (see p.174, Section 5 'Exercise Physiology'). This is especially important in slow, prolonged work. Anaerobic energy production (energy produced when oxygen is not available to the cells) is intermittently used whenever fast work or extreme power is required, such as in multiple jumping efforts or powering up hill stretches during competition. All competition horses require a basic level of aerobic conditioning however, whatever their sport, in order to compete effectively.

Feeding tactics
There is no one-size-fits-all feeding regime for competition horses, and a great deal depends on the temperament and condition of the individual horse.

Nutrient Focus

The following are key nutrients for competition horses (and see page references to Sections 4 and 5, given where relevant):

Water

Always offer during travelling and at the competition, to prevent dehydration (see p.146).

Energy and Protein

Although some horses have too much energy, it pays to keep an eye on the sources of energy (see p.148), as these fuel both exercise and recovery. Protein, and specifically the amino acid lysine, needs to be in balance with energy, in a ration of 10g protein and 0.35g of lysine per megajoule of energy consumed.

Energy Sources (and see p.148)

Fibre, starch and oil are the main energy sources in any horse's diet. Using fibre and oil to generate energy aerobically at low speeds conserves glucose for when it is needed most. In addition, both these nutrients can replace starch in the diet reducing the risk of dietary upset through the overfeeding of starch. High starch levels may also contribute to exuberant behaviour.

Electrolytes (and see pp.146 and 164)

Exercise, sweating and horses that fret all require electrolyte, or more specifically, rehydration therapy, a combination of water and electrolytes. Less than 2 per cent dehydration affects performance and if not spotted, slows recovery times.

Antioxidants (and see p.168)

As the muscles generate power, so various waste products are formed that require removal. Tissue-damaging free radicals are amongst the more harmful examples that are generated under stress, and antioxidants 'mop up' free radicals. Between 1–2,000 ius of vitamin E, and up to 3mg per day of selenium, are a good benchmark here.

A Horse that Works On Little Feed

Some competition horses look good and perform well on very little feed, even when competing at high levels: any more, and the extra hard feed will affect their behaviour – they become silly or stroppy – or will lead to unwanted weight. Plenty of horses competing in advanced classes eat no more than 2–3 slices (4–6kg (8–13lb)) of hay, and 2–3kg (4–6lb) of a low energy feed. With such a diet, energy and protein levels will be below published requirements, though this is not an issue provided that all nutrients are in balance, and that micronutrient supply (see p.162) is at requirement. With horses that put on weight easily, it can be tempting to limit their forage to prevent them gaining unwanted pounds, but this increases the likelihood of stereotypical behaviours gastric ulcers and colic (see pp. 136, 126 and 116, in Section 4); a minimum safe fibre level is 1 per cent of bodyweight, ie 5kg (11lb) of hay (8kg (17lb+) haylage) for a 500kg (1,000lb) horse.

Typical feed rates for competition horses *(see also Section 2, 'Practical Feeding')*

Novice	2–3kg (4–7lb) low energy or competition feed, plus hay and/or grass (minimum 5kg (11lb)).
Intermediate	3–4kg (6–9lb) competition feed, hay and/or grass (minimum 5kg (11lb)).
Advanced	5–6kg (11–13lb) competition diet or high energy feed (or a mixture of both), forage minimum 5kg (11lb).

Of course, amounts will vary according to the height, weight and temperament of the individual horse or pony.

The Worrier

Some competition horses eat up well at home or before the season starts, but once competitions are under way they go off their feed, and consequently lose weight as the season goes on. Feeding tactics here are more about managing the horse to give him regular breaks – though obviously it is also important to find a feed that he will eat, and to use that.

Wear and Tear

All athletes' bodies are subject to above-average levels of stress, and horses that have been competing over several years will suffer from the usual wear and tear. Special feeding regimes are necessary here. If long-term muscle problems are the main issue, then the horse's chances of recovery are improved if a high fibre, high oil, and low- or no-starch diet is fed. If it is joints and stiffness, then some joint supplements do seem to 'free up' horses well, although they cannot reverse existing damage.

Non-nutritional support also includes the close attention of the back specialist and physiotherapist.

Feeding the Older Horse or Pony

Horses, like humans, become old at different ages. Horses are classed as 'aged' when they are over nine, although this is universally accepted as a young age nowadays. It is a common perception that a horse is 'elderly' when it reaches sixteen years of age, but there are many examples of horses competing at the highest levels, such as at the Olympics, at the age of sixteen or over.

A good guide is that if a horse shows no sign of its age, then it isn't necessarily a candidate for an 'old age' feed. Like humans, however, the population of older horses is increasing. **This is due to:**

❑ the keeping of horses into retirement, rather than destroying them when their useful working life is over;

❑ better management and medical care of the horse throughout its life, and advancements in veterinary care and treatment;

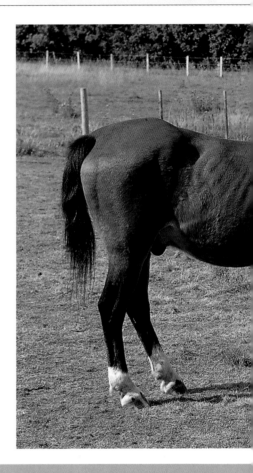

Nutrient Focus

Research into the nutrient requirements of older horses has been carried out, but it is not wholly comprehensive.

Protein

An average working horse will require about 10 per cent protein in the diet. The older horse requires between 12 and 14 per cent in order to maintain better muscle and body condition. It is important that the protein is of good quality in order to avoid stress to the liver. The essential amino acid profile should be good quality.

Phosphorus

Phosphorus retention is reduced in the elderly horse, mainly through a reduction in fibre digestion. Reduced phosphorus retention is also a feature of those horse and ponies suffering Cushing's disease (see p.120).

Fibre

Fibre sources should be high in digestible fibre such as cellulose and hemicellulose, and low in indigestible fibre such as lignin, especially if horses have poor or no teeth. Straw should only be fed in moderation, as should hard hay,

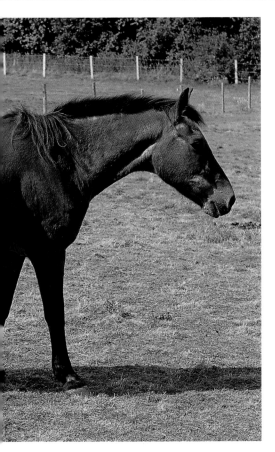

the availability of improved worming programmes, thus reducing the number of horses that die from worm-related problems;

improved horse dentistry and better availability of dentists.

Feeding Tactics

Continually check the teeth

❏ Monitor the horse's ability to chew his food. Inadequate chewing of food can lead to quidding (the spilling of feed from the mouth), poor feed utilization, and colic.

❏ Horses and ponies with poor teeth should be fed a high fibre feed soaked to a mash, which allows easy uptake and minimal grinding before swallowing.

Monitor the horse's condition
Monitor the horse's ability to withstand work
Feed for the work done

❏ See p.55, Section 2 'Rules of Good Feeding'.

Feed a veteran feed to an oldster

❏ For a horse that is no longer able to hold his condition on normal low energy feeds use a veteran feed. Recommended levels of veteran feeds are typically as follows:

Ponies: Between 1–3kg (2–6lb) a day.
Horses: Between 2–5kg (4–11lb) a day.

Check laminitic horses

❏ Older horses and ponies prone to laminitis, such as those with Cushing's disease (see p.120, Section 4) should only be fed higher nutrient-density veteran or conditioning feeds in small quantities. These ponies' diets should be based on high fibre, low energy feeds that can be fed safely in large quantities.

in order to reduce the risk of impaction colic. Dry feeds should be fed with care, as the risks of choking will be increased. If teeth are worn or missing, cubes should be fed soaked.

Cooked cereals

It is essential that everything in a diet for an elderly horse is highly digestible. Digestible fibre and oil make good energy sources, and any cereals should be offered either flaked, micronized or boiled so as to facilitate easy absorption and to reduce the likelihood of the overflow of starch into the hindgut.

Feeding the Brood Mare

In temperate climates, mares will begin to ovulate – 'come into season' – naturally from April to November. Reaching peak fertility is driven by day length – lengthening daylight hours stimulates a reduction in the hormone melatonin, which in turn triggers a cascade of hormonal activity culminating in ovarian activity. This also coincides with an increase in the amount of grass, and therefore the quality of nutrition, which also drives fertility; for instance the beta-carotene in grass is known to exert a beneficial effect on the quality of the egg produced. In Thoroughbred breeding farms the understanding that the onset of oestrus is driven by day length often allows manipulation of its start by the use of lights and improved nutrition.

Once pregnant, the gestation period for a mare is 11 months, typically ranging between 335 and 345 days for Thoroughbreds, and slightly less for other breeds, though again, this varies with the day length at the time of foaling. Most of the foetal growth occurs in the final three months of pregnancy.

On foaling, the mare produces milk at a rate of between 3–5 per cent of her bodyweight, an enormous metabolic effort. After about 3–4 months the quality and quantity decrease as the foal becomes more reliant on other feedstuffs.

Mares are also regularly sent back to the stallion whilst with a foal at foot, and so can be both pregnant and lactating at the same time – although the metabolic demands of mid- to late lactation and early pregnancy are not onerous.

Feeding Tactics for the Pregnant Mare

Early pregnancy

❑ For the first eight months of pregnancy the mare can be fed at maintenance, although the opportunity should be taken at this time to increase the condition of a poor mare or to control further weight gain in overweight mares.

Late pregnancy

❑ During the last three months, the growth of the foetus increases nutrient requirements by up to 20%, whilst at the same time the capacity of the mare to eat large quantities diminishes. For mares foaling in May and June, the required increase in nutrient density can be underpinned by good grass; but mares foaling between January and April, or those on poor pasture, will require some form of stud feed, at between 30–40 per cent of the daily ration. (Native pony mares may not need the extra energy and protein that these feeds provide; probably all they require are extra amino acids and micronutrients, and a breeding supplement will provide these.)

Lactation

❑ During early lactation, the mare's metabolism will produce milk at any cost. Any reduction in feed energy intake below requirement means that she will lose condition, as she will generally 'take it off her own back' in order to generate energy for milk production; a situation than can be harmful if not addressed quickly. As with the late pregnant mare, the time of year dictates the feeding regime. Mares foaling between January and April, or those consuming hay or haylage diets, will require significant quantities of stud feeds (up to 60 per cent of the daily ration) to provide the significantly increased requirements for milk production. Mares foaling in May and June will benefit from the high quality of grass at this time, and will require less hard feed, with perhaps only a supplement for particularly good doers (easy keepers) to make good any shortfalls in the grass micronutrient levels.

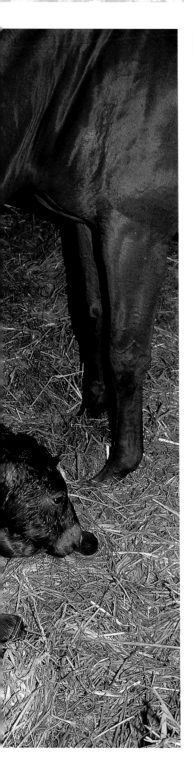

Nutrient Focus

Water

Intake can double during lactation, therefore a supply of clean fresh water should always be available.

Energy

Requirements rise significantly, to almost double the levels required for mainte-nance, to fuel growth and milk production. The graph shows the increase in energy requirement for a 500kg (1,000lb) mare.

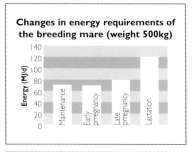

Changes in energy requirements of the breeding mare (weight 500kg)

Protein

Requirements increase to supply the neces-sary amino acids for milk production and growth in the foal (see graph).

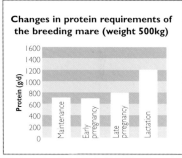

Changes in protein requirements of the breeding mare (weight 500kg)

Micronutrients

The mare's requirements also increase in line with energy and protein. To a certain extent these are met by the increased intake of highly nutrient-dense feeds at this time, but the concentrations of calcium and phosphorus in particular rise, due to their role in bone development and milk production. Intakes increase by up to three times the levels required for maintenance as a result. The following table indicates the difference in dietary concentrations of these two elements:

	Dietary calcium content (g per kg of diet)	Dietary phosphorus content (g per kg of diet)
Maintenance or light work levels	3.2	2.0
Mare in late gestation and when lactating	5.5	3.0

Feeding the Stallion

As it is with mares, increasing day length stimulates fertility in stallions, and so they are at their most fertile during the spring and summer. The increase in a stallion's nutrient requirements above maintenance depends on his workload: if he is competing, the number of mares he must cover, how well he holds his condition, and his temperament.

Feeding Tactics

❑ Given that the uses of stallions are many and varied, and they are essentially working when covering mares, choosing an appropriate feeding regime is more akin to feeding the working horse (see p.53, Section 2: Practical Feeding). Fat stallions are less agile, however, and may be less comfortable when covering mares; they are also at risk of developing laminitis, especially those of native blood.

Nutrient Focus

Extra energy and protein

These are needed to meet the increased demands of working. The average Thoroughbred stallion requires in the region of an extra 20 MJ of energy per day above resting levels, as well as an extra 165g (6oz) of protein per day.

Mineral and vitamins

The requirements rise: Vitamin A is directly involved in sperm production, although lack of this vitamin is extremely rare, especially in breeding-horse diets. Vitamin E supplementation has frequently been used to increase fertility, although whether it is effective in this role has not been directly proven – it is more likely to be linked to its role as an antioxidant. (See also p.46, 'Supplements' and p.168, 'Antioxidants'.)

Feeding Youngstock

Feeding a youngster from weaning at 4–7 months into adulthood, without problem, is some challenge. Certainly native youngstock left to grow naturally on hillsides do not develop the same problems of over-excess as fast-growing Thoroughbred or warmblood breeds, but they will be subject to nutritional challenges of a more traditional deficiency kind.

Statistics show that up to two-thirds of Thoroughbreds do not ever make it to the racetrack or withstand training, much of which is related to early bone development (see Section 5, p.176). Management and genetics therefore both play as great a part as nutrition in the production of a healthy adult.

Nutrient Focus

Energy and sources of energy
See Section 5, p.148.

Mineral and vitamins
See Section 5, p.162, 170.

Feeding Tactics

Monitor growth and development of youngsters on a day-to-day basis

❑ As growth is a dynamic process that varies with the individual, you may have to alter the amount and type of feed given as the horse grows. Growth rates vary according to the season and the forage quality, but a smooth curve of growth gives greater bone strength than a regime that varies with the time of year.

It is also highly probable that fast growth rates precipitate bone problems, so planning a moderate growth rate (see Section 5, p.176) is likely to reduce their incidence. This may not be achievable, however, if the value of the youngstock is based on their appearance in a sales ring at foal or yearling stage, as prospective purchasers currently favour large, well grown types at any age.

Feeding weanlings

❑ A suitable youngstock or creep feed should be fed at around 450g (1lb) per day for each month of age until the youngster is 8–9 months old. After this, the feed rate can be dropped to around 225g (½lb) per month of age. This kind of product is generally suitable for feeding until a youngster is two years old. Depending on growth rate and the individual circumstance, it may be that in a youngster's second summer, ie when it is 12–18 months old, much less of such a feed is required.

Feeding Natives and Native Cross-breeds

❑ Stud rations are often too rich for breeds that evolved to live off poor quality grazing, besides which these breeds usually foal in the summer when most of the nutrition for the foal and weanling can be obtained from grass. A standard low energy cube or mix (sweet feed) is often sufficient to provide the energy and protein these breeds require, and the additional micronutrients can be supplied by a breeding supplement.

Feeding the Orphaned Foal

It is always a great tragedy when a foal is orphaned, but swift action is necessary to ensure its survival without the mother. The first aim is to find a surrogate mother, but failing that, foals can still be reared successfully by hand, and with patience and effort can be raised to become the archetypal happy and playful little horse.

Nutrient Focus

Growth rate in the new foal

Such is the rate of growth in a new foal that the nutrient requirements, particularly for energy, are about 3½ times greater than for an adult horse for maintenance. The foal is reliant in its first weeks on the milk of the mare, or in the case of the orphan, the milk replacer, to provide its complete nutrition.

Feeding Tactics

Feeding weanlings

❑ Colostrum is the so-called 'first milk' from the mare, produced between twelve and twenty-four hours after birth; it contains the essential antibodies necessary for the foal to be able to develop a healthy immune system with which to fight disease. The foal loses its ability to absorb these immunoglobulins within a few hours of birth, and so it is essential to feed colostrum immediately to prevent the foal succumbing to disease. If mare's colostrum is not available, then there are several commercially prepared colostrums available.

Make hygiene a priority

❑ Cleanliness is next to godliness with rearing foals, as they are susceptible to infection and disease. It is essential to have clean buckets and utensils, and to clean down the stable (preferably steam-clean it).

Train to suckle

❑ The suckling reflex is also lost early in the foal's life, and must be established within the first few days of its life. Once a foal has learnt to suckle, it can then be trained to drink from a bucket.

Feed every two hours at first

❑ Then feed four-hourly until the foal is about

Milk replacers

- ❏ Mare's milk replacers come in dried, powdered form ready for mixing, and are the preferred choice. However, if they are unavailable, alternative milks can be used (see below).
- ❏ Cow's and goat's milk can be used, but they are richer than mare's milk and should be diluted 50:50 with skimmed milk to achieve a similar nutritional content to mare's milk.
- ❏ Milk pellets based on cow's milk are also an alternative, providing high protein (20–25 per cent) and high fat (12–15 per cent) for fuelling growth.
- ❏ Calf milk replacers have been used successfully in foals, but they should contain at least 20 per cent protein and 15 per cent fat.
- ❏ Lamb's milk replacers are more concentrated and less suitable.

a month old, then three times a day after that. Feeding large amounts at once increases the likelihood of diarrhoea or colic.

Follow the manufacturer's instructions

- ❏ With commercial milk replacers, use the correct proportion of powder to water: 10–15 per cent dry matter is the ideal; more concentrated mixtures may cause constipation.

Make changes gradually

- ❏ Increase the amount of milk offered gradually. Solid feeds such as milk pellets can be offered in small amounts early on: foals can, and will, eat about 225g (½lb) per day of such products,

in addition to milk in their first two weeks of life, rising to 1kg (2lb) by eight weeks. You can wean a foal around this time. Once weaned, a foal's consumption of dry feed will increase rapidly to 2–3kg (4–7lb) per day.

Don't spoil the foal

- ❏ It is human nature to overprotect, but the helpless little foal will soon turn into a larger young horse. Foals accustomed to such privileges as *ad lib* titbits and treats may become awkward to handle when a little later you wish to take a more disciplined approach to training.

Feeding the Racehorse

The racehorse is a pure athlete, whether he is bred to gallop on the flat – sometimes at speeds up to 40mph (64kmph) – or to stay longer distances and run over fences in a hurdle race or steeplechase. He will also be competing at different ages, the flat-race horse from two years of age, and the National Hunt horse from his fourth year.

Whilst feed and feed strategy are of great importance, much of a horse's performance in a race is due to its innate ability, its stage of fitness, and the ability of the trainer and jockey. There are, however, some feeding principles worth following: these are shown opposite.

Nutrient Focus

Energy

The primary requirement in these horses is for energy, although their requirement for all nutrients is increased. The blend of sources of energy depends on the feeds used, the distances over which the horses run, and the skill of the head lad (See 'Energy' p.148).

Racehorse diets are traditionally based on starch (being based on oats), but modern racehorse feeds now have high oil and high fibre options (See Section 5 pp150–7.)

Electrolytes

Racehorses also have increased requirements for electrolytes, to replace those lost in sweat (see also p.146 and p.164).

Feeding Tactics

Monitor dust in feed

❑ Minimal dust feedstuffs are required: any obstruction to the airways through respiratory irritation or infection will impair performance. (See p.138, Section 4 'Recurrent Airway Obstruction'.)

Keep forage to a minimum and hard feed to a maximum

❑ In racehorse diets, forage is the lowest energy component of the diet and is therefore kept to a minimum, with the hard feed at a maximum. A high energy compound feed and/or oats are typically used as the hard feed.

Feed the forage of choice

❑ The traditional forage for racehorses, seed (hard) hay is very low in nutrients, and is used to maintain gut function with little nutrition expected from it. Also given that forage binds water within the digestive tract, and that 1 litre (2 pints) of water weighs 1 kg (2.2lb), large forage intakes are avoided to minimize excess weight. Certainly in the UK, premium quality seed haylage is more frequently the forage of choice in racehorse diets. (See p.28 and 30, Section 1, 'Forages'.)

Typical feed rates:

FORAGE
Hay 4kg (8.7lb) Haylage 4–6kg (8.7–13.2lb)
COMPOUND 6–8kg (8.7–17.6lb)

The amount eaten depends on:

❑ the age of the horse;
❑ its sex (fillies tend to eat less);
❑ its size;
❑ its health status;
❑ the stage of its training: horses in full training can lose their appetite.

These figures reflect what is typically fed, and are below the textbook 2.5 per cent target for a horse in hard work.

Feeding Box-resting Horses

It can happen at any time – an injury or attack of disease that causes the horse to be confined to its stable for a period of time. It is always a challenge to feed these equine inmates – frequently they are at peak fitness when injury or disease hits, so not only are there physical considerations, moving them off a high plane of nutrition and feeding for repair and recuperation, but there is also the mental challenge of keeping a fit horse, that is now 'confined to barracks', sane. Horses can become depressed, and usually lose a lot of condition in the first few days and weeks of box rest, and this needs to be re-established during the recovery phase.

Nutrient Focus

Fibre

Essential for healthy gut function, and critical in the horse on box rest. Move rapidly to a low energy, high fibre, low starch diet. This will help maintain a healthy gut, keep an excitable horse calm, and reduce the risk of azoturia, laminitis and colic (see Section 4, p.116 and 118).

Energy and protein

This might sound like a recipe for disaster in the box-resting horse, but both are essential for repair of tissue. It is not the amount that is critical – no one could sanction feeding high energy and protein feeds to a horse in no work – but the ratio of energy to protein is

important, and more specifically, the supply of the amino acids lysine, threonine and methionine (see Section 5, p.159), to make sure they are all available for repair. Energy and protein are also the drivers of condition. One veterinary hospital and referral practice I know prefers to feed a medium energy, high fibre competition-type feed to this kind of horse, as they say the extra calories in these feeds both help with condition, and supply enough energy to prevent depression.

Vitamins and minerals

In box-resting horses, the minerals and vitamins that are provided from forage will not always

What can and can't be done will depend on the condition that caused the need for box rest.

Feeding Tactics

Walk the horse out in hand each day if practicable

❏ Let him graze – the more the better. This very light exercise helps the horse mentally because it provides variety, it helps prevent stiffness, and the movement will help to expel excess digestive gases built up over the day: these can contribute to colic in the inactive stabled horse.

Supply plenty of food

❏ The horse needs plenty of food for nourishment and so that the horse can occupy up to 60% of the day eating (the amount of time he spends eating naturally).

❏ Change to a high forage diet – a continuous supply of good quality forage will keep a stabled horse well occupied.

❏ Hay or short-chop forages that take longer to eat are used in preference to haylage, to reduce any dietary excuse for stereotypical behaviours developing (see Section 4, p.136).

Feed bran mashes tactically

❏ Although much maligned (see Section 1, p.38 and p.142), this is the most practical way to bring a horse swiftly from a high to a low energy diet. Bran has energy and protein contents more akin to competition feeds than hay and a decent fibre content. A one-off mash makes for a good transition for the rapidly immobilized horse changing to maintenance or recuperation rations.

Feed high fibre, low starch feeds

❏ These provide the necessary vitamins and minerals together with energy and protein to supply nutrients for recuperation.

Stabilize the horse before trying to restore lost condition

❏ Condition can be improved in time by using a conditioning feed at 50 per cent of the hard feed, or alternatively using a balancer or other conditioning supplement at 200g (7oz) to 1,000g (2lb 3oz) per day, depending on the product.

be present in sufficient quantity for effective repair of damaged tissue. If no compound feed is given, or only low levels, then a general purpose vitamin and mineral supplement will supply the extra micronutrients (see Section 1 'Supplements', p.49). This can be offered mixed in with the daily feed, or mixed with a bit of chop, chaff or sugar-beet pulp if necessary.

Digestive aids (see Section 1, p.50) such as yeasts, although not always scientifically proven in horses, act to support a healthy gut environment, and therefore can be beneficial in some cases, especially when restoring gut function after surgery or large-scale antibiotic use.

Feeding to Put Weight on a Horse

In the wild, weight gain and loss follows a seasonal fluctuation according to the availability of food. The horse stores body fat during the good times (spring, summer and autumn) and uses these stores when food is less available during the winter.

Most horse owners notice weight loss at the onset of winter as daily temperatures drop, grass growth slows and its nutritional value falls. Outwintered horses and ponies require about 30 per cent more energy to keep warm during the winter (less if they are rugged and stabled), and extra feed energy is required. Feeding plenty of hay at this time not only provides nutrients, but generates heat through the fermentation of fibre in the hindgut, which will help keep the horse or pony warm.

There may, however, be other times when a horse's condition falls below target, and the following is given as a checklist to run through before amending any feeding practices:

- ❏ Check the teeth (see Introduction, p.10): sharp edges may be causing pain or discomfort and a reluctance to eat.
- ❏ Check the worming programme: in unwormed horses, feed often provides nutrition for the worms rather than the horse, and so they must be removed. Veterinary surgeons and wormer manufacturers provide advice on the best products to use.
- ❏ Check for any pain in the musculoskeletal system that may be affecting the way a horse carries itself.
- ❏ Check for other disease, especially with rapid weight loss.

Nutrient Focus

Energy

For weight gain, the focus is on the supply of additional energy, and its sources (see Section 5, p.148.) Starch is traditionally the preferred form of increased energy; however oil, being energy rich, is a more concentrated energy source (Section 5, p.156).

Protein

Conditioning feeds are generally high in protein, which supplies the amino acids that are necessary for muscle development (see p.158). Excess protein will also be used as an energy source.

Feeding Tactics

Assess the weight and condition of the horse

❑ Assess the weight and condition of the horse, and calculate the total amount of daily feed based on 2.5 per cent bodyweight. For example: a 500kg riding horse will require 12.5kg of total feed per day, equivalent to four slices of hay and either three standard scoops of cubes, or four standard scoops of mix (sweet feed).

Increase forage intakes

❑ Turn out onto good grazing or offer hay or haylage *ad libitum* if the horse is stabled. If the grazing is poor, hay or haylage should be given in the field.

Feed more of the exisiting hard feed.

❑ Often poor condition is reported in horses and ponies receiving very small amounts of hard feed, and the simple action of increasing feed from 1 to 3kg (2.2 to 6.6lb) per day (gradually) often makes a difference.

Use a conditioning feed.

❑ Conditioning feeds are designed to put weight on horses and ponies and are very effective. These are high energy, nutrient-rich feedstuffs containing quality protein, and can be fed on their own or on a 50:50 basis with the usual hard feed.

Typical feeding levels of conditioning feeds	
Small native breeds	0.5–1.5kg (1.6–3lb)
Large native breeds	1–2kg (2–4lb)
Small horses up to 15hh	1–3kg (2–6lb)
Large horses up to 16hh+	2–4kg (4–8lb)

Feed balancers and milk pellets

❑ These are both highly nutrient-dense forms of feed that work as conditioning supplements, providing weight gain without causing excitability in a low dose (between 250g–1kg (½–2.2llb) per day). These products can be used with any feed from a low energy upwards.

Use barley and linseed

❑ Boiled barley and linseed are traditional conditioning feeds. The energy from barley is more efficiently converted into body fat than that from oats, and boiling cooks or gelatinizes the starch within the grain, making it more digestible to the horse. Linseed is energy and protein dense, and the process of boiling here removes poisonous constituents (see Section 1, p.40). Boiled barley, like other high starch foods can cause excess excitability in horses.

Weight gain for the show ring

Another often controversial situation when weight gain is required is that for putting on increased condition in show horses and ponies, over and above that which might be considered normal. In these animals, condition is synonymous with topline, where it is a common misconception that increasing feed can put muscle on a horse. What the feed does do is provide the nutrients and protein required for muscle development, but the producer needs to provide the exercise and schooling to build up the muscle tone.

Feeding to Lose Weight

Some breeds or types seem to pile on the pounds at the drop of a hat, and others maintain condition on very meagre diets: the latter are signs of the 'good doer' (easy keeper). Breeds most likely to put on weight are the native breeds, such as Irish draught horses, cobs, cob crosses and Arabs.

Encouraging a horse to lose weight is slightly different from keeping weight off once it is lost. As with humans, weight is most effectively lost when both feed energy intake and exercise levels are addressed simultaneously. Starving is not the answer, either. Complete removal of energy from the diet causes a condition known as hyperlipaemia, which is in effect excess fat in the blood, and is harmful to the horse.

Very low intake diets can also cause behavioural problems in horses that have become very hungry: barging and general bolshiness is not uncommon (see Section 4 'Stereotypical Behaviours', p.136). For these reasons it is best to aim for a slow, rather than rapid reduction in weight.

Nutrient Focus

Energy

Calories must be controlled, but not removed altogether. Reducing the daily diet to 1.5 per cent of the bodyweight can reduce the energy intake by 30–40 per cent over an unrestricted diet, which, combined with exercise, should be effective. Clearly for less drastic weight loss, less of a reduction in feed per day will work.

Vitamins and minerals

Horses and ponies on a weight loss programme will require vitamins and minerals, especially if grazing is restricted (see Section 5 'Minerals', p.162 and 'Vitamins', p.170). Provide a general purpose supplement in these cases, either fed directly or mixed with a little feed (see Section 1, 'Supplements', p.46).

Feeding Tactics

Establish the horse's weight

❑ When a horse is in target condition (see Section 2, p.57), it is usual to work on 2 per cent of bodyweight as a guide to the total amount of feed, but for weight loss, work on between 1.5 and 2 per cent body-weight, depending on how much weight is to be lost. For example, a 350kg (770lb) pony on a diet should be fed 350kg (770lb) × 1.5% = 5.25kg (11lb 8oz)/day of total feed; this is equivalent to two typical slices of hay (4kg/8lb 13oz) and 1.25kg (2lb 12oz) of a low energy feed. These are small amounts: be aware that this can be about 3kg (6lb 12oz) less per day than the diet of an equiv-alent size animal of poorer condition.

Restrict grazing

❑ Grass is a high energy feed, especially in spring (see Section 1 'Grass', p.22 and Section 4 'Laminitis', p.118).

Add a broad-spectrum supplement when low levels of concentrates are fed

❑ This ensures that micronutrient requirements are met (see Section 1 'Supplements', p.49).

Use feeding stuffs that are as high in fibre and low in energy as you can for the level of work undertaken.

Feed the equine dieter separately

❑ If feeding with other horses outside, the animal on the diet will finish first and raid other horses' feeds.

Measure feeds by weight, not volume

Increase the exercise

❑ Especially for those horses that don't get much. When ridden, keep them up to the bit. Alternatively plenty of trot work, for instance on the lunge, will help.

Be patient

❑ Excess weight can be hard to budge, and will take some time to come off. Slow, steady progress will not stress the horse or cause digestive upset.

Once target weight or condition is achieved, move the amount fed back up towards the 2 per cent of bodyweight level.

Move to the diet feeding regime gradually, over 7–10 days.

Have regular weigh-ins: a weightape, although not 100 per cent accurate, will give a good indication of progress.

4 Diet-related Ailments and Feeding Myths

In this section

❑ Poor performance   114

❑ Colic   116

❑ Laminitis   118

❑ Equine Rhabdomyolosis Syndrome (ERS)   122

❑ Gastric ulcers   126

❑ Allergies and intolerances   128

❑ Ailments associated with growth   130

❑ Choke   132

❑ Liver damage and disease   134

❑ Stereotypical behaviours   136

❑ Recurrent airway obstruction   138

❑ Common feeding myths   140
  Sugar in a horse's diets
  Feeding bran
  Performance boosters boost performance

Poor Performance

Not every diet-related ailment manifests itself in a disease or condition: sometimes poor performance, whether generally or during a particular event, is a manifestation of either a more widespread problem, or a temporary dent in optimum nutrition. Poor performance is not all down to the feeding and nutrition of a horse; but some basic physiological measurements may help determine the cause, and whether nutrition has been implicated. In this situation, check the following parameters:

- ❑ **Training level**: Were you and the horse fit and able to undertake the performance target?
- ❑ **Underlying physiological irregularities**: eg heart irregularities.
- ❑ **Lameness**: Is there any observable or subclinical lameness present, and where is it – legs, back, muscles?
- ❑ **Respiratory system:** Is the horse suffering from a respiratory tract challenge or airway obstruction?

Have your horse's teeth checked regularly

(See also this section p.138.)

- ❑ **Diet:** Is this the best it can be for the horse, for what is required of it? (See also Section 2, in particular pp.58–61.)

A review of feeding is an essential dietary check and involves measuring what the horse actually eats and drinks, not what is offered. For example, many performance horses offered *ad libitum* (free-choice) hay, tread it into their bedding. This information can be checked through a nutritionist's rationing programme to check for any imbalances. Individual feedstuff analysis may be called for to investigate particular issues (see Section 1, p.35).

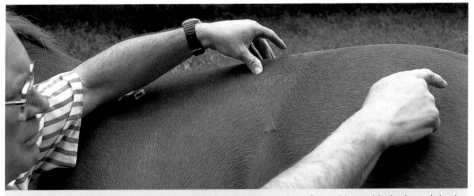

Ask you veterinary surgeon to check that there is no sign of a problem with the horse's back

Blood and Urine Tests

These are commonly used as a diagnostic tool but are best used in conjunction with other information such as rider feedback and physiotherapists reports.

Disease
Blood count: white blood cell levels

Fitness or muscle problems
Blood enzyme levels, particularly CK (creatine kinase) and AST (aspartate aminotransferase), liberated from muscle cells when damaged. Their continued presence in blood post exercise or episode of ERS indicates the rate, or otherwise, of recovery.

Nutritional deficiencies

❑ Chronic energy and protein worries
Blood urea and blood proteins

❑ Electrolyte status
Urine tests*, analysis of the diet

*A fractional electrolyte excretion test will indicate electrolyte status. High excretion indicates a surplus supply; low excretion, a deficiency. Focusing solely on serum electrolyte values instead might lead to wrong nutritional interpretation, and an ineffective revised diet. Low blood status does not necessarily reflect chronic deficiency of an electrolyte – what is more likely is a hydration status issue, which could in turn be linked to fibre levels in the diet. Using dietary analysis and a fractional electrolyte clearance test in addition to blood tests enables a fuller picture to emerge.

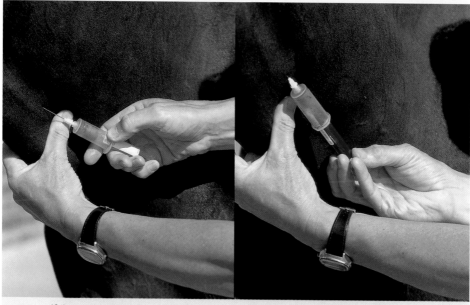

If the problem cannot be readily detected your vet may take a blood sample to be tested

Colic

Colic is the most common medicinal problem of adult horses. It is a pain in the abdomen usually associated with distension of the gastrointestinal tract. It is highly likely that most horses suffer an attack of colic on several occasions through their lives, but of a mainly mild form. In more severe forms a vet should be called at the first sign.

Classic symptoms of colic are:
- ❑ General restlessness
- ❑ Horse turning its head to look at abdomen
- ❑ Pawing the ground
- ❑ Kicking at the abdomen
- ❑ Sweating
- ❑ Raised pulse and respiration rates
- ❑ Rolling

Rolling: a classic symptom of colic

Diet and Feed Management

Colic is mainly a horse management issue, and feed guidelines are as follows:

❑ Keep worming up to date to reduce the risk of parasite-induced colics.

❑ Teeth should be checked regularly to ensure correct mastication of food and thus reduce the risk of impaction.

❑ Follow the rules of good feeding (see Section 2, p.55).

❑ Allow horses that are stabled for prolonged periods some exercise, either in hand or in a loose school, to encourage movement of any gases that have built up in the digestive tract.

Feeding Tactics

Colic		Causes
Spasmodic colic	The vast majority of colics appear in this form, caused by spasms of the intestinal wall that last for a relatively short time.	❑ A sudden change in diet, to a higher energy diet or high starch feed. ❑ General chilling of the horse, including large ingested amounts of cold water soon after strenuous work. ❑ Worm damage by migrating larvae. ❑ Increase in general stress due to travel or a change in surroundings.
Impaction colic	Accounts for 30% of colic cases, and is, as the name suggests, the result of a blockage, usually in the large intestine.	❑ Horses with poor teeth, preventing proper chewing of feed. ❑ Eating bedding and other highly lignified coarse forage. ❑ Inadequate water supply or failure to drink, eg through unpalatable water. ❑ Hard work and associated sweat losses.
Sand colic	Relatively rare but recurrent form, requiring liquid paraffin to remove.	❑ Large consumption of sand or mineral matter either through accidental uptake on sandy soils, or through habit-related eating of soil.
Gas colic	The horse produces about 150l (33gal) of gas per day that is either expelled or absorbed into the blood. Build-ups in the digestive tract cause extreme pain and sometimes its rupture.	❑ Failure to expel gas that builds up throughout digestive tract during digestion. ❑ Can be caused after consumption of rich diet, lush grass or grass cuttings. ❑ Often a secondary feature of impaction colic.

Laminitis

Laminitis is most frequently seen in fat native ponies in the spring months, but can occur in other horses at any time. The causes of laminitis are these:

- Diet, especially compounded by under-exercise.
- Toxaemia and fever, most commonly as a result of retained placenta in mares after foaling.
- Traumatic, from concussion to the feet from trotting hard on the roads, or continual jumping on hard ground.
- Veterinary drugs; cortisone can cause rapid-onset acute laminitis in rare cases. High doses of thiabendazole, used in some wormers, has also been implicated.
- Extreme stress: the horse produces high natural levels of cortisone, which is thought to induce laminitis.
- Cushing's syndrome (see p.120): laminitis is often seen as a secondary symptom.

Laminitis results from a lack of blood flow to the laminae of the foot, resulting in internal swelling and fluid build-up, leading to pain as pressure develops in the enclosed hoof area. In extreme cases, the pedal bone within the hoof can rotate and sink, and can even push through the sole of the hoof (also known as solar prolapse). It is a painful and debilitating disease, and to prevent it in high risk horses requires active management.

Dietary Management of the Laminitic or Laminitis-risk Horse

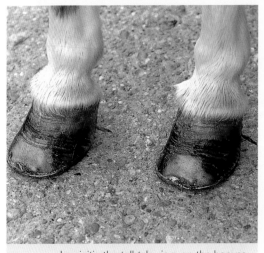

Laminitis: the tell-tale rings on the hooves

- Feed a high fibre, low carbohydrate, low energy diet.
- Limit grass (see Feeding Myths, Sugar in a Horse's Diet, p.140) and use hay or a hay replacer as the forage. Feeds accredited for laminitics are available on the (UK) market. Those fed just hay or hay replacers will benefit from some form of micronutrition in the form of a supplement or balancer (see p.49).
- Use other animals to eat down grazing land, or top the pasture regularly to remove excess growth. Laminitis-risk horses and ponies need only very little grass.
- Put overweight ponies or horses on a diet (see Section 2 p.64, also p.110).

The typical stance of a horse suffering from laminitis:the weight is shifted onto the back feet

Nutritionally Induced Laminitis

70 per cent of laminitis cases occur amongst horses on pasture in periods of rapid grass growth. Preparation for the show season also precipitates some cases if large amounts of high-starch feeds are fed in an effort to gain the often hefty show condition that judges want. Causes include:

❑ Excess carbohydrate in the diet from sugar, in spring and autumn grass, and starch, from high cereal and coarse mix (sweet feed) intakes.

❑ Obesity: in fat ponies and show animals, and in under-exercised and over-fed animals in general.

Laminitis is often common during the first frost of winter. This has led to the development of the fructan theory: that when plants are 'stressed' by temperature fluctuations, plant carbohydrates are stored as long chains of fructan sugars: these are indigestible in the small intestine. Similar chains are also common in short 'bare' pastures that have been 'stressed' by trampling and over grazing. It is thought that these fructan sugars are fermented in the hindgut, rather like excess starch, the ensuing disruption being the cause of laminitis.

Cushing's Syndrome

Also known as hyperadrenocorticism, pituitary pars intermedia dysfunction (PPID), or Cushing's disease, this is a syndrome caused by a tumour of the pituitary gland of the brain, which produces a number of hormones that control a wide range of body functions.

As a result of the widespread impact of the pituitary hormones on body function, a variety of symptoms are recognized, of which one is a sudden, unexpected onset of chronic laminitis that then reoccurs. This form of laminitis is difficult to treat, as it does not have nutrition as its foundation. Diagnosis of Cushing's syndrome is via raised blood cortisol concentrations, and blood sugar and fat measurement.

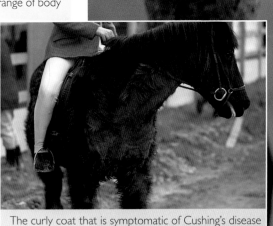

The curly coat that is symptomatic of Cushing's disease

Symptoms of Cushing's syndrome are these:

❑ Long curly coat, failure to shed winter coat and patchy sweating.

❑ Excessive thirst – consumption of up to 80l (17gal 4.75 pints) per day.

❑ Increased appetite for no weight gain.

❑ Chronic laminitis.

❑ Pot-bellied appearance.

❑ As cortisol depresses the immune system, increased susceptibility to illness.

Feeding strategies are similar to that of the laminitic but for different reasons: a high fibre, low starch and low sugar diet is recommended, with additional antioxidants (see p.168) to support immune function.

The link between fructan levels

...asture and laminitis is the subject of ongoing investigation

Evaluating the fructan risk

The recent research linking fructans and laminitis has posed more questions than it has answered. In terms of practical management of horses in relation to the fructan risk, it is easy to forget basic laminitis-avoidance management. The work proposing the link between fructans and laminitis has been developed from work done in humans and rats, and as yet has not been proven directly in the horse. Fructans are said to be highest in stemmy grasses, in cool conditions – but this is most likely to occur in late summer, not universally known as a laminitis-risk period.

Fructan levels in typical horse pasture have not been studied, and whilst more research will undoubtedly be done in this area, the current level of knowledge does not allow accurate feed management strategies regarding fructans for laminitis-prone horses.

Short, tightly grazed horse pasture is unlikely to contribute large amounts of fructan to the diet, as intakes will be relatively low on these pastures. In addition, the stalky material that may contain more fructan later in the summer is not as succulent as fresh spring grass, nor grows as fast, and so the rate of consumption will be considerably less, so reducing the risk.

Remember, the more a horse eats, the faster the food travels through the digestive tract, so giving less time for digestive enzymes to get to work in the small intestine. Therefore it might not be fructans *per se* that cause a spring attack of laminitis: rather, it is more likely to be the total oversupply of nutrition that rapid grass growth supplies, with excsess sugars ending up in the hindgut.

Equine Rhabdomyolosis Syndrome

Azoturia, tying up, exertional rhabdomyolosis, setfast, Monday morning disease, exertional myoglobinuria, polysacchardide storage myopathy (PSSM), and also recurrent equine rhabdomyolosis (RER): all are names given to a variety of muscle conditions that currently fall under the banner of equine rhabdomyolosis syndrome (ERS).

Fundamentally, what occurs in ERS is serious tissue-level damage to muscle fibres in, usually, the large muscle masses, in the croup, loins and thigh areas. This damage impairs the ability of the whole muscle to function correctly, and the severity of an episode varies in degree, ranging from mild stiffness and shortened stride, to the extreme where the affected muscle groups become hard and painful, and render the horse unable to move. A classic sign of the condition is discoloured, dark red urine, as damaged muscle protein (myoglobin) is excreted via the kidneys. Horses also become anxious, and sweat profusely, and have elevated pulse and respiration rates during an episode.

ERS is categorized into sporadic and chronic forms. 'Sporadic' indicates horses that suffer intermittently from the condition, and 'chronic' repeated attacks in the same horse from early on in its career. Also to be considered is muscle damage caused by over-exertion, as the signs of this are the same as for the chronic form. 15 per cent of horses in a recent study showed signs of muscle damage from over-exertion, and so this as a 'cause' of a suspected attack of ERS cannot be ruled out.

In ERS serious damage to the muscle fibres occurs, sometimes as a result of over-exertion

Sporadic ERS

The sporadic form is often associated with horses suffering an episode after a day off on full rations. Oversupply of hard feed, undersupply of forage and hormonal imbalances are all implicated here. Dietary or sweat-induced electrolyte insufficiency can also predispose a sporadic ERS episode, as electrolytes are crucial in muscle function (see p.164). Clinical or subclinical illness can also predispose a horse to a sporadic attack, and an unexpected attack of tying up is often the first sign of illness in a yard.

Chronic ERS

Chronic ERS is itself split into two distinct subtypes. First, recurrent exertional rhabdomyolosis (RER) occurs as a result of an inherited defect in muscle contraction common in Thoroughbred and Arab breeds; as many as 5 per cent of Thoroughbreds are affected. It manifests itself particularly in fillies, and it seems that nerves and excitability are both trigger factors, as are high cereal diets.

The second sub-type is polysaccharide storage myopathy (PSSM), also inherited, but completely different from RER as it involves excessive storage of carbohydrate in muscle fibres. It is most prevalent in Quarter Horses, but can also be found in warmbloods, and some Thoroughbreds. Rest is a trigger factor, because it allows for the massive accumulation of muscle carbohydrate.

The massive build up of carbohydrate in muscle fibres in Quarter Horses makes them particularly prone to attacks of chronic ERS

Diet and Feed Management

Clearly the overall management is crucial, but nutrition has a vitally important role to play, through energy and electrolyte supply, and in the reduction of excitable behaviour. Critical in all cases is to move away from cereals as a source of energy. Some PSSM horses require a no-starch diet, but all ERS horses will benefit from controlled rather than zero-starch diets.

Oil is often suggested as a replacement energy source to starch (see p.165), but the maximum amount that can be fed is about a kilo, and so other forms of energy are required, such as digestible fibre.

Feeding the Sporadic Case

❑ This is predominantly about day-to-day attention to detail in horse and feed management, analysing forage (see p.35) for electrolytes, and cutting the feed, or moving to a low-energy product on days off, or during periods of enforced rest (see pp 60 and 78).

Feeding the RER Case

❑ A two-fold strategy should be adopted that controls excitability and starch levels. Excitability can be managed by reducing or removing any stimuli or excuses, changing the stabling so the horse can see others, and altering the exercise routine. Changing from a high cereal diet reduces the effect that rapid release of starch and sugar has on temperament, and prevents issues of starch overload into the hindgut. High oil, high fibre feeds are a good alternative. (See pp. 56, 84 and 148.) Electrolyte levels should also be maximized.

Feeding the PSSM Horse

❑ Feeding strategy here is to prevent carbohydrate build-up in the muscles, combined with management that allows only short rest periods, on an all-fibre diet. For horses in work, a very low starch and sugar diet is essential (see Section 2 pp58–61): conserved forage (not grass, which is high in sugar) (see 'Forages' p.22), with high fibre and high oil compounds.

Feed and Management Strategies to Minimize the Risk of ERS

❑ Keep forage levels as high as possible for the work being done.
❑ Use feeds based on fibre and oil, with controlled starch levels.
❑ Limit intakes of unsupplemented cereals, as these are high in starch and have a low mineral and vitamin content.
❑ Increase the workload before increasing feed levels to prevent the unnecessary build-up of carbohydrate in muscle.
❑ Decrease hard feed on days off by 50 per cent or more, or move to a low energy feed.
❑ On a daily basis warm up slowly, especially after a day off, and keep horses' muscles warm, especially in winter if the horse is clipped.
❑ Turn the horse out as much as possible.

Gastric Ulcers

It has been reported that 80–90 per cent of horses in training, and a significant number (up to 50 per cent) of competition horses have gastric ulcers. It is not that these are a new phenomenon, however; rather, the increase in reported cases reflects improvements in diagnosing their existence.

The core of the issue is that the equine stomach is designed to receive feed on a little-and-often basis, and as a result the secretion of highly acidic digestive juices, the first step in the digestive process, takes place continuously in anticipation of a more or less constant influx of food material. Acid is produced in the lower part of the stomach, an area that is designed to cope with the production of strong acid. The upper half of the stomach does not produce acid, nor does it have protection mechanisms if acid does come into contact with it. However, discrete meals are the opposite to the system that *Eohippus* learnt to live by. Whilst the acid is produced continually, it is only required four or five times a day, during meal times.

Saliva, a natural buffer to acid, is only produced when a horse chews, and inevitably a horse chews more on a diet high in forage, than one that is high in compounds. Therefore the diets of competition horses and racehorses, where forage is limited and compound intakes high, will not produce large quantities of saliva, and this means less ability to buffer stomach acid. The physical mixing effect produced by any active movement or jumping, will then create conditions where acid comes into contact with the unprotected area of the stomach, and ulcerative damage will occur.

Diet and Feed Management

Since ulcers are a condition of low fibre, high grain diets, any shift back towards a more natural diet will reduce the incidence: gastric ulcers disappear once an affected horse is turned out to grass, so daily turnout will mitigate against ulcers forming. Sadly, this isn't always feasible for horses in training; however, until horses can chew for longer than the time that three meals per day and two slices of hay allows, ulcers will form. (See also p.62.)

Antacids

Antacids treat the symptoms, rather than address the root cause, and there are several products on the market that act either to reduce the amount of acid produced in the first place, or to neutralize the stomach acid produced. Antacids aren't a cure, however, but they do act to reduce the risks associated with low forage, high concentrate diets. The only real cure is to organize the diet so that it is as natural as possible.

Indicators of gastric ulcers are:

❑ General irritability
❑ Loss of appetite
❑ Poor condition

However, these symptoms are not unique to the condition and gastric ulcers may be present in horses that show no signs.

Blood-test results can show:

Chronic low iron status as a result of persistent blood loss from ulcers.

Competition horses have been shown to be particularly at risk of developing gastric ulcers if their diet is not managed with care

Allergies and Intolerances

In most human diets, food allergies and intolerances receive plenty of headlines in the health press, and the same is becoming true in the horse world, with a great many products and preparations available for the management of the horse with an allergy or intolerance. However, true allergic reactions are very rare in the horse population, as diagnosed by blood tests for the agents of inflammatory response. Such allergies are usually a response to a particular protein in the diet, rather than the total amount of protein supplied.

'Hives' or bumps under the skin are a relatively common indication of an intolerance to food. This may be due to overfeeding as much as to a reaction to a particular ingredient.

Allergies can occur all over the body, or in isolated areas such as the back or head,

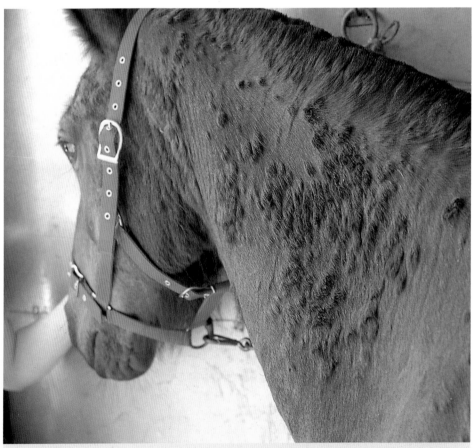

Urticaria: an allergic reation that may occur with a sudden change in diet

or they may cause the horse to rub his mane and tail.

In treating allergies, veterinary surgeons usually recommend steroids to control the inflammation, together with removal of the cause. Once sensitized, a horse can remain susceptible for many months, or even a lifetime, depending on the severity of the reaction. In some cases, what is initially thought of as an allergic reaction may actually be the early signs of another disease or condition, and so careful monitoring of the horse is recommended. While allergies do not cause raised temperatures or fever, horses suffering from a viral infection do on occasion develop lumps, in addition to other more recognized symptoms. The early stages of ringworm also may be interpreted as an intolerance.

Diet and Feed Management

Protein

Protein is often implicated in allergies. Cereal proteins in particular are most likely to trigger a reaction. Significant overfeeding of protein, or a lack of magnesium (see p.163) in the diet (both quite uncommon), can also lead to allergy-like reactions due to higher circulating blood urea levels.

Barley or wheat proteins are the most likely cereals to be implicated, but the other cereals can also produce a response. Removing flaked cereals from the diet may not have the required effect, as both cubes and the mineral and vitamin pellets in coarse mixes (sweet feeds) will contain fibre-rich cereal by-products – so products declared as 'allergy free' will be nothing of the sort if they contain cereal by-products. (See also 'Protein' p.158.)

Molasses

Molasses have never been implicated in scientifically determined feed-related allergies, but lumps developing in horses on highly molassed feeds have from time to time been reported.

Physical symptoms

Irritation from feedstuffs can also produce intolerance-like symptoms, and usually affect all horses on a yard, rather than one. Forage or bedding mites are a common source of allergy and irritation, from hay or straw. Hives around the face and neck implicate hay, and this can be alleviated by feeding the hay from the floor, or those over the belly and legs suggest straw, and this can be alleviated by replacing the straw with fresh material or another bedding material, after a thorough clean-down of the stable.

Exclusion diets

A typical exclusion diet for horses suspected of having an allergy or intolerance involves removing cereals from the diet. A diet based on grass, or a non-straw-containing forage replacer (see p.34), together with a limestone-based supplement, is a suitable base (see also 'Supplements' p.46).

Ailments Associated with Growth

Developmental orthopaedic diseases (DOD) are, as their name suggests, conditions of bone that occur during development, their net effect in adult horses being to affect bone strength, quality, and ultimately soundness. DOD is just an umbrella title for a number of disorders in young horses that interfere with normal bone development, also known as dyschondroplasia. At its heart is the failure of cartilage to fully develop into bone, resulting in a weakened structure. It is prevalent in fast-growing breeds such as Warmbloods and Thoroughbreds, appearing particularly in the hock and stifle, and less often in the fetlock and shoulder. Its incidence as a disease is estimated at 15 per cent in growing horses, but the effects of subclinical or unidentified lesions on the soundness of horses once in work is significantly greater. Most of these developmental diseases are triggered by four factors:

- Genetics: above all this determines the speed of growth;
- Conformation: which determines the way a horse moves, and therefore the likelihood of lameness;
- Trauma: through excessive concussion;
- Diet.

Diet and Feed Management

The following policies should be observed:

- Limit high-energy diets: these are strongly related to the incidence of developmental bone diseases, and fuel high growth rates. For instance, fast-growing families seem to suffer osteochondritis dissecans (OCD – defective development of bone from cartilage, resulting in inflammation in the affected joints) more frequently than horses or families that develop more slowly. (See also 'Energy' p.148.)

- Control starch: research has shown that high starch diets, fed in large, discrete meals, can be detrimental to bone development. Youngstock reared on mainly grass diets do not suffer the same rate of DOD as those stabled and fed discrete meals. (See also 'Carbohydrates' p.150.)

- Focus on micronutrients: this must be balanced with the energy density of the diet. Key micronutrients in growing horses are calcium, phosphorus, copper, zinc and manganese, all involved in bone and cartilage metabolism. Deficiencies of copper and zinc, and induced deficiencies of calcium in particular, can cause OCD (see pp. 49 and 162), although correcting such deficiencies will not prevent the condition if excess high-starch feeds are offered.

Risk to fast-growing horses

Fast-growing horses are most at risk, as bone development takes place rapidly. Research has shown that bone is not as dense under high-speed growth conditions, compared to that which matures more slowly.

Fast-growing horses, such as these, are at risk of developmental diseases without careful feeding

Choke

There is nothing more distressing than a case of choke to both the owner of the horse and the horse itself. Choke is the common name given to oesophageal impaction, or dysphagia, caused by obstruction of the oesophagus with food or a foreign object. It is not common, but it can recur in horses that have suffered a previous attack.

All choke obstructions require veterinary assistance, not only to free the material, but also to assess the level of damage to the oesophagus, and to check that no feed matter has entered the lungs. Whilst the feed itself may be the cause,

Regurgitation of saliva seen in a case of choke

The most common signs of choke are:
- ❑ difficulty in swallowing;
- ❑ making frequent but ineffectual attempts to swallow;
- ❑ retching movements;
- ❑ signs of distress;
- ❑ drooling;
- ❑ some reguritation of food or saliva through the nostrils in long-standing cases;
- ❑ visible lump in the gullet where the obstruction lies.

Diet and Feed Management

- ❑ Seek veterinary help: the horse may need tranquillizing, and perhaps stomach tubing.

- ❑ Try and keep the horse as quiet as possible.

- ❑ If the choke is only slight, offer the horse soft, soaked feeds (hay and hard feed), and a pick of grass. It is essential that he eats something, both to minimize digestive disturbances and to keep up the flow of saliva, as saliva contains chemicals that aid repair of damaged tissue.

- ❑ If more severe, the horse may be kept off food for up to seventy-two hours, and then offered only soaked feeds.

- ❑ A horse that has had a prolonged oesophageal obstruction may well be dehydrated. Offer water and electrolytes once the obstruction is clear.

Management for the Prevention of Choke

❏ Check the horse's teeth regularly.

❏ Feed hard feeds with chop or chaff to slow down the rate of eating and to encourage mastication, or put large stones in the bottom of the bucket to slow down the horse's speed of eating.

❏ Place the feed at floor level (see p.63, Section 2, box: 'Keeping Horses Happy').

❏ If soaking (not damping) feed, ensure that all sugar-beet pulp nuts and pellets are broken down. This takes at least half an hour for pelleted feeds, and longer for sugar beet (at least half a day).

❏ Allow a horse to eat in peace, avoiding any commotion that may cause him to move from the manger to the door rapidly; alternatively, you could place a 'busybody' horse's manger near to the door.

❏ With a horse prone to choke, feed all feeds soaked.

usually choke occurs as a result of a combination of factors.

In foals, choke may be the result of immaturity, disease or, in rare cases, a congenital deformity. In youngstock, erupting teeth may mean that food is not masticated properly, and this can predispose a horse to choke. In older horses, choke can be caused by poor teeth, by improper chewing or rushing of the food, and by lack of water. The latter two affect the production of saliva and the ability of the horse to lubricate the food bolus as it enters the digestive system.

The feeding activities of a greedy horse, one competing for feed, or excitable horses that take one bite of feed and rush to the front of the stable, may all result in feed not being chewed properly. In each case feed that has not been broken down into fine particles is swallowed, often without enough of the lubricating saliva, and this can cause choke.

If it is related to feed, the bottom line is that food is swallowed too soon, or not chewed properly, either due to poor teeth or rapid consumption. Don't forget, though, that some horses are predisposed to choke, having a natural stricture of the oesophagus.

Liver Damage and Disease

The liver is the central metabolic 'hub' of the body, and fulfils various roles: it processes energy and protein, detoxifies metabolic waste, stores nutrients and metabolizes nutrients such as glycogen, vitamins A, D and B12 and copper, and manufactures the digestive secretion, bile that is responsible for an optimum digestion environment in the small intestine.

Liver disease produces biochemical changes to the liver without an obvious sign of disease; however, it can be helped by supportive management. Liver failure results in clinical disease, and occurs when the metabolic functions of the liver are seriously impaired (usually when more than 80 per cent of liver cells have been destroyed). The long-term prognosis in such cases is poor.

Signs of liver disease
- ❑ Loss of appetite
- ❑ Weight loss
- ❑ Jaundice
- ❑ Photosensitization of skin, especially on the muzzle and on white markings
- ❑ Manic walking
- ❑ Depression
- ❑ Yawning
- ❑ Head pressing (this indicates a severe case; once a horse does this, the prognosis is poor)
- **Blood tests** can confirm the diagnosis, via increased serum alkaline phosphatase (ALP), aspartate aminotransferase (AST) and sorbitol dhydrogenase (SDH).

Ragwort and liver damage

Of the many plants poisonous to horses, the one they are most likely to consume is ragwort. This and other toxicants, such as heavy metals and some mycotoxins, can cause liver damage. In the case of ragwort poisoning, the poisonous principle, pyrrolizidine alkaloids, accumulates in the liver and halts its regeneration. Liver disease is becoming increasingly common, mostly due to the rapid increase in the amount of ragwort in and around horse pastures in Britain. Ragwort is most dangerous when dead or dying, as it is generally unpalatable when growing. Hay or haylage that is made from ragwort-contaminated land is therefore high-risk material, and all bought-in forages should be checked accordingly. (See also p.66, Section 2 'Poisonous Plants'.)

Dietary Management

The dietary strategy should concentrate on lowering the metabolic workload of the liver; it should aim for:

❑ Low protein: aim for 8–10 per cent in the total diet. Avoid leafy hays and haylages (cut before mid-June), all pasture, alfalfa or dried grass products, soya bean meal and linseed, and high-protein compound feeds. (See also p.158.) Seed hays and haylages or oat straw blends are recommended

❑ Low oil: avoid large (>150ml) additions of oil to the diet (although the addition of a small amount of cod-liver oil may be beneficial in providing the fat-soluble vitamins A and D). (See 'Fats and Oils', p.156.)

❑ High-soluble carbohydrate from starch and sugars: this helps to maintain constant blood glucose levels without the liver having to mobilize glycogen and fat stores. (See 'Carbohydrates', p.150.)

❑ Vitamin supplementation: of vitamins A, D, E and B12, as liver stores will be poor. (See pp. 49 and 170.)

❑ Branched-chain amino acids: essential amino acids required in energy transfer, and available from veterinary surgeons, or in special liver disease diets. (See also 'Protein' p.158.)

❑ Horses with liver disease tend to lose condition; however, don't be tempted to feed large amounts of conditioning feeds immediately, as these tend to be high in protein. Judicious use of varying ratios of the above feeds will work, but it is best to request advice on the individual circumstance from a vet or nutritionist.

❑ Feed little and often: this in itself will reduce the metabolic workload of the liver. (See p.65.)

A practical 'off-the-shelf' diet could include:

Hay, particularly seed hay
Low energy, low protein, offered *ad libitum*.

Sugar-beet pulp
Soaked: it adds sugar and digestible fibre and tempts a fussy feeder.

Low energy cubes, high in fibre
Low energy and low protein feed.

Cooked, flaked barley or maize
High starch-containing feeds

General purpose supplement
Provides a balanced supply of micronutrients.

Stereotypical Behaviours

Research has shown that an increase in the time spent not feeding results in an increase in abnormal behaviours; previously these were known as stable vices, but now they are acknowledged as stereotypical or abnormal behaviours, defined as '...methods by which horses cope with the stresses of an unnatural environment.'

Whilst feeding management is not the only cause of stereotypical behaviours, there is plenty of evidence to show it plays a part. Feeding discrete meals in the same way that we eat ourselves is unnatural to the horse: we forget they have evolved over thousands of years to be 'trickle feeders', eating little and often, and a horse with nothing to do may adopt a stereotypy such as crib-biting, wind-sucking and weaving to cope. (See also p.62, 'Feeding for a Contented Horse'.)

Restricted feeding facts

❑ A stabled horse on a low forage, high concentrate diet may spend less than 15 per cent of its time eating.

❑ This means the horse has as much as half a day of 'free' time to fill.

❑ Feeding less than 7kg (15lb 7oz) of forage per day is associated with the development of stereotypical behaviours.

❑ In one study, over 30 per cent of dressage and event horses showed abnormal behaviour.

Dietary Management

❑ Keep forage supply above four slices of hay (8kg) per day, or preferably offer *ad libitum*.

❑ Feed forage in several small nets provided throughout the day.

❑ If this is not possible, use other sources of fibre such as low energy forage replacers (see p.34), that take longer to eat (typically 1kg (2.2lb) takes 1 hour to eat).

❑ Feed forage replacers in full buckets: a standard bucket typically contains 1kg (2.2lb).

❑ Hard feed should be given in three or four feeds per day if possible.

❑ Consider using a stable toy (that may or may not dispense feed or treats) to occupy the horse.

❑ Allow access to other horses, both sight and touch.

❑ Where possible use straw as a bedding; higher incidences of stereotypical behaviours have been observed on other bedding types.

❑ Increase exercise or turnout times.

Crib-biting: when forage is restricted a horse may be forced to find other ways to cope with the stress of confinement

Recurrent Airway Obstruction

This is the newest term for what was previously known as 'chronic obstructive pulmonary disease' (COPD), and is the most frequently seen equine respiratory disease. It is a disease of the lungs of horses similar to asthma and farmer's lung in humans, in that it is a hypersensitization and inflammatory reaction in the small airways of the lower respiratory tract to certain moulds and filamentous bacteria. A somewhat less severe but similar condition is 'inflammatory airway disease' (IAD).

Although there is some evidence of genetic predisposition to such hypersensitivities, environmental factors are by far the most frequent causes.

Signs of COPD are:
- ❏ Chronic cough
- ❏ Nasal discharge
- ❏ Laboured breathing
- ❏ Inability to sustain any kind of workload

Hay and, to a lesser extent, bedding are the prime sources of the moulds that cause such hypersensitivities. The mould species associated with COPD are *Aspergillus fumigatus* and *Micropolypora faeni*: both of these grow in warm conditions, as do the highly allergenic filamentous bacteria,

the *Thermophilic actinomycetes*.

Such conditions do not generally exist during normal hay-making, and only arise if the baled hay is subsequently poorly stored in the barn; therefore a sunshine-filled hay-making season does not automatically guarantee low-mould hay. Despite most of the water having been driven off as the grass dried in the field, a residual amount remains within the bale that naturally evaporates in storage. It is good practice to store newly made hay in barns allowing plenty of airflow between bales, between rows in the stack, and between the stack and the walls of the barn. Any failure to do this results in the hay heating up as microbiological activity re-commences, and the end result of such heating is hay contaminated with allergenic mould and bacterial species. Unfortunately, only in severe cases is this contamination visible.

Not all hay is affected in this way, or poses such risk, however; much hay grown in damper, temperate climates has some dust associated with it from moulds that have colonized the grass as it lay in the field. These are non-allergenic, though if present in huge numbers could cause some form of respiratory allergy.

Dietary and Management Strategies

There is only one solution, and that is to create a non-allergenic environment for the horse:

❑ Minimal dust environment, comprising well ventilated buildings to circulate air and prevent dust in the atmosphere.

❑ Soaked hay or haylage, or dust-extracted hay replacers (see also p.22, Section I 'Forages').

❑ High-fibre compound feeds have also been proven as low dust hay replacers if none of the above are suitable (see p.42, Section I 'Compounds').

❑ Stabling during high pollen season; otherwise increased turnout away from enclosed atmospheres.

Soaking hay to remove spores from the grass or cause them to stick to it

Common Feeding Myths

Sugar in a Horse's Diet: Acceptable or Not?

The rise in awareness of nutrients in relation to human nutrition has an impact on the way we consider feeding our horses, and particularly in relation to the sugar in their diet. However, there is a world of difference between the dietary supply and the needs of man and horse in this respect.

The horse evolved to live on grass and other pasture plants that are all high in sugars, and it is efficient at utilizing sugar, which is broken down to glucose and digested in the small intestine. Little sugar reaches the large intestine unless the horse experiences a sudden change in diet, such as turning it out onto rapidly growing spring grass.

Nevertheless, as a general rule a horse or pony grazing on spring grass can take in large quantities of sugar without a problem. For example a 16hh, 500kg (1,000lb) horse is able to eat 12.5kg (28lb) (dry matter) of grass a day: with a sugar content of up to 5 per cent in grass dry matter, this means an intake of 2.5kg (5.5lb) of sugar per day, equivalent to two and a half bags of sugar!

Although grass contains a relatively high percentage of sugar, exactly how much is dependent on other factors; for instance:

❑ The weather: sunshine and high temperatures mean high sugar levels, as the plant converts carbon dioxide from the atmosphere into sugar.

❑ Grass species: ryegrasses and new grass seeds have the ability to make more sugar than traditional meadow grasses.

❑ The time of year: spring grasses contain more sugar than later season growth, which contains more lignin.

Spring grass contains more sugar than later season growth

Sugar in a Horse's Diet

The following table indicates the sugar supply to a 350kg (770lb) Welsh-type pony, doing Pony Club activities (light/medium work), out at grass in the summer and stabled with hay in the winter. By way of comparison, a bag of sugar weighs 1kg (2.2lb), and a teaspoon 5g, so the intakes have been expressed in bags or teaspoons of sugar.

The total sugar supply here is 1,290g (2.8lb), or just under 1½ bags of sugar per day. Over 77 per cent of this comes from the grass. (For the sugar content of various equine feedstuffs, see table p.152, Section 5, carbohydrates.)

Typical summer diet			
Feed	Intake in kg (lb)	Sugar supply	Tsp/bag equivalent
Grass	**35 (77)**	**1,000g (2lb3oz)**	**1 bag**
Cool Mix	**1 (2.2)**	**90g (3oz)**	**18tsp**
Molassed chaff	**0.5 (1.1)**	**100g (3.5oz)**	**20tsp**
Molassed sugar-beet pulp	**2 (4.4)**	**100g (3.5oz)**	**20tsp**

Typical winter diet			
Feed	Intake in kg(lb)	Sugar supply	Tsp/bag equivalent
Hay	**6 (13.2)**	**150g (5.2oz)**	**30tsp**
Cool Mix	**1 (2.2)**	**90g (3oz)**	**18tsp**
Molassed chaff	**0.5 (1.1)**	**100g (3.5oz)**	**20tsp**
Molassed sugar-beet pulp	**2 (4.4)**	**100g (3.5oz)**	**20tsp**

Here, the total sugar supply is 440g (15.5oz), just under half a bag of sugar per day, and about a third of the summer intake. In this diet, 35 per cent comes from the hay and 65 per cent from other feeds. Remember also that these intakes are spread over twenty-four hours, so that on average a pony consuming this diet would be eating about 3–4 teaspoons per hour (0.3g/minute) when stabled, or 11 per hour (1g/min) at grass.

Cases When Sugar Should be Limited

While sugar *per se* is not harmful, as an energy source digested in the small intestine, over-supply or sudden increases of sugar are not recommended. For horses or ponies prone to laminitis, a low sugar strategy has a role in lowering the intake of soluble carbohydrate, to reduce the risk further. Remember, though, that this will only be effective if the diet as a whole is high in fibre and low in starch as well.

Ways to reduce the sugar level in a horse's diet

Action	Reduction in sugar level
Restrict grazing to 3hr/day; feed hay instead	minus 846g (30oz)/day
Feed low-sugar coarse mix (5% instead of 9%)	minus 45g (1.6oz)/day
Feed low-sugar chaff (10% instead of 20%)	minus 10g (0.3oz)/day
Remove the molassed sugar-beet pulp	minus 100g (3.5oz)/day
Replace with unmolassed sugar-beet pulp	minus 72g (2.5oz)/day

Feeding Bran: What are the Benefits?

Bran receives either a good press or a bad press, but nothing in between. Some say it is the root of all evil, others say it has been an integral part of a horseman's dietary repertoire since time immemorial, and so can't be all that bad.

Bran is one of the by-products of flour production and consists of the outer, fibrous layer of wheat unwanted in the finished floury product. Traditionally this and other, similar products have been used in animal feed because, while it wasn't a 'natural' for human diets, it was thought to be of great use in animal diets – in fact the modern animal feed industry evolved to use up the by-products of the human food industry, and this is one such example. (See also p.38, Section 1 'Bran'.)

Over the years, however, the milling process has changed, and old nagsmen bemoan the passing of the 'broad bran' of twenty years ago. Modern-day bran is much finer, and those who have known the former, refer to today's version as sawdust – but this is to ignore its benefits. A quick run-through of its nutritional characteristics shows it to be quite nutritious in the major nutrients. It has an energy content similar to medium-energy feeds, and a protein content of 14 per cent (although to be fair, the quality of this protein is not as good as that, say, of soya). Bran contains less fibre (12 per cent) than forages, but more than most traditional compounds with its energy content, and

Bran – good or bad? Opinions are divided

being cereal-based, is highly palatable, which means it is a useful tool for tempting a tired or fussy horse to eat – and for concealing medicines.

Bran is traditionally fed as a mash (see p.38, Section 1) on the horse's day off, and in doing this, feeders take advantage of the fibrous energy it contains. The broad bran of old was capable of absorbing large quantities of water, and so acted as a laxative in speeding the passage of food through the digestive system. Feeding a wet bran mash is a canny way of combining the intentions of rehydrating the horse, and maintaining a fair amount of energy in the diet with fibre, rather than starch, so reducing the risk of digestive upset.

However, bran lost its appeal not only due to the change in its physical form, but also because of its poor calcium content. Like all cereals and cereal by-products, the calcium content is negligible, and the phosphorus content relatively high by comparison. This is the opposite of what it should be for the horse, which requires a ratio of twice as much calcium to phosphorus in its diet, for optimum absorption and retention of calcium within the body. Feeding large amounts of bran can distort the balance of these two elements, and a calcium supplement, such as limestone, should always be fed if you are feeding more than 1–2kg (2.2–4.4lb) of bran at any time.

Performance Boosters Boost Performance

There are many products available that promise enhanced physiological function in horses, be it enhanced immune response, blood boosting, or delaying fatigue – or any one of the hundreds of other claims out there. The validity of such claims can only be backed up by research, of which, despite there being a growing body of equine physiological trials to lean on, there is little in respect of performance enhancement. In addition, a horse's performance is not totally reliant on its nutrition and physiology, and none of the research around suggests that its genetic potential can be overridden by a dietary supplement.

There are two basic rules to apply if assessing whether a particular product is the one for you:

❑ **Does the explanation as to its effect sound plausible?**
Always ask the manufacturer for their explanation, and be determined not to accept vague answers to specific questions.

❑ **Does it work?**
Ask for the evidence that it works, both in science and in field trials. Anecdotal reports of it working in individual cases may not mean that the product will work for you.

Clearly the decision to purchase a nutritional aid depends upon the price of the product relative to the claim, and the value the purchaser has for the promised improvement.

5 Nutrition Fundamentals

In this section

Knowing the layout of the digestive tract is only the beginning of the understanding of nutrition. If the digestive tract is the site where ingested food becomes body fuel, then the 'fuel' is in the form of soluble nutrients.

A nutrient is defined, somewhat obviously, as a substance that provides nourishment, and to study nutrition means to study the supply, absorption and modes of action of nutrients. The principle elements of nutrition are: water; carbohydrates; fats and oils; vitamins; minerals.

❑ Water 146

❑ Energy 148

❑ Carbohydrates 150

❑ Oils and fats 156

❑ Protein 158

❑ Minerals 162

❑ Vitamins 170

❑ Physiology in perspective 172
   Exercise physiology
   Growth physiology

Water

Water is essential to all known living organisms: none can exist without it, and most known organisms consist of a large percentage of water – for instance, a foal consists of up to 80 per cent water, and a mature horse 65 per cent water. Most of this water is in the cells of the body and in the digestive tract, as well as being a major component of blood.

Water is often overlooked in favour of the 'solid' nutrients such as carbohydrates, fats and protein; however, whilst not truly classed as a nutrient, its importance in fact transcends all others. Its main importance is as a transporter, supplying nourishment in the form of the other nutrients in the

High heat and humidity

A horse may need to increase its water intake by over four times to cope with high heat and humidity.

blood and within the cells of the body.

Generally speaking, a horse usually consumes more water than it needs. Exactly how much water an individual horse will drink each day is difficult to predict, as this will vary depending on the moisture content of the feeds it eats, its workload, and the day-to-day climatic conditions.

With so much water contained within the body, it is not surprising to learn that

Water Checklist

❑ Even small levels of dehydration will affect a horse's performance: 2 per cent (10kg in a 500kg (22lb/1,100lb) horse) will affect performance, and this is below the level the common 'pinch test' will detect.

❑ Allow frequent small drinks when exercising. In a recent promotion by a human sports drink manufacturer, human athletic performance was improved by 30 per cent by the regular consumption of the sports drink throughout an exercise test – primarily through the maintaining of hydration status.

❑ Water drinkers are convenient, but unless metered, you do not know how much a horse is drinking. Water supplied in buckets is more labour intensive, but it is easier to monitor intake that way.

❑ Horses that are poor drinkers often don't perform well. Tips for tempting poor drinkers include sweetening the water with sugar-beet pulp liquor, honey or molasses.

❑ Alternatively a moist, sloppy feed is another good way to get water in, especially when travelling, where such a feed may be more appealing to a horse in a moving horsebox than a bucket of water.

❑ Water from a private source should be checked for quality from time to time: local authorities or the Environment Agency will do this. Chemical analysis checks the content of minerals and chemicals, both good and bad, for which there are prescribed limits. Microbiological analysis will look for the presence of harmful organisms such as coliforms that may indicate the presence of dead animal matter in a water tank.

In the field, the horse will regulate its own water intake

it doesn't stay put in one place for long. On eating a meal, blood flow is diverted to the digestive system to facilitate the transport of nutrients absorbed from there. This redistribution of blood is in addition to the influx to the gut of digestive juices that aid digestion: it has been estimated that up to 100 litres are added during digestion. It is for this reason that one of the rules of good feeding states not to work soon after feeding – with fluid shifted towards the digestive tract, it is likely that the horse will be dehydrated peripherally.

Energy

Second in importance to water is energy. Again, whilst not truly a nutrient, it is of major importance to the horse as fuel. The processes of life require energy as their fuel, and the energy horses use comes from the oxidizing of carbohydrate, fat and, to a lesser extent, protein, from their diet or from their own body stores. To most of us however, energy conjurs up mental images of athletic endeavour; and equally, energy in a feedstuff is taken to mean its capacity to excite a horse, or to put weight on. These effects are more to do with the source of energy and its release, than energy *per se*.

Every feed contains energy, some more than others, depending on their composition. It is almost like a hidden nutrient because it cannot be measured directly as can other nutrients such as protein. The energy content is calculated from its chemical components, so that the carbohydrate, oil and protein levels in a feed all contribute to its energy value.

In the UK, the form of energy used to describe feeds and horse requirements is digestible energy. The unit of energy measured is the megajoule (MJ). In the USA, digestible energy is also used, but the units of energy used are calories. Calories and joules can be easily inter-converted by the factor 4.18:

1 calorie = 4.18 joules, and 1mcal (1,000,000 calories) = 4.18 MJ (megajoules)

Common feedstuffs, their energy content, and their principal energy sources		
Feedstuff	Energy content	Sources of energy
Grass	High	Sugar, protein and fibre
Hay	Low	Fibre
Haylage	Low/medium	Fibre, sugar and some protein
Oats	High	Starch
Sugar beet pulp	Medium	Fibre, sugar
Vegetable oil	High	Oil
Low energy cube	Low	Fibre
Low energy mixes	Low	Fibre, starch
Competition cube	Medium/high	Starch, oil and some fibre
Competition mix	Medium/high	Starch, oil and some fibre

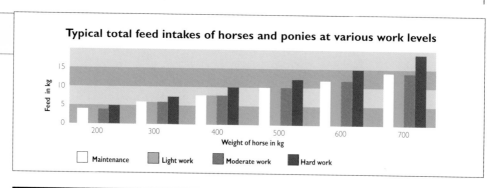

Typical total feed intakes of horses and ponies at various work levels

Feed in kg

15
10
5
0

Weight of horse in kg

200   300   400   500   600   700

☐ Maintenance ☐ Light work ■ Moderate work ■ Hard work

Grass: a source of high levels of sugar, protein and fibre

Oats: a feedstuff with a high energy content

Carbohydrates

Carbohydrates are the collective name given to the starches, sugars and dietary fibres that can be digested in some form to provide energy. A horse is essentially a carbohydrate converter, since typically its diet is comprised of up to 80 per cent carbohydrate. In human nutrition, carbohydrates are classified as either monosaccharides, disaccharides or polysaccharides, depending on their complexity; the monosaccharides and the disaccharides are the least complex, being comprised of sugar molecules in singlet or doublet form. Polysaccharides are known as 'complex carbohydrates' as they are more complicated structures. Amongst the polysaccharides are starches and certain fibre components of the diet. In horse nutrition, the distinction is simplified further, in that carbohydrates fall into one of two categories, structural carbohydrates and non-structural carbohydrates.

Feedstuff	Fibre content (crude fibre, %)
Grass	10–20
Hay	30–35
Haylage	30–35
Straw	38–42
Alfalfa	25
Oats	10
Barley	5
Low energy cube	14–20
Low energy coarse mix (sweet feed)	10–15
Sugar-beet pulp	13
Bran	11

Structural Carbohydrates

The term 'structural carbohydrate' encompasses dietary fibre, and describes those carbohydrates that confer 'structure' to plants, or give a protective coat to seeds as plant cell walls and associated compounds. Fibre itself is a compound made up of a mixture of different complex carbohydrates (or polysaccharides), including cellulose and hemicellulose, bound together with some non-carbohydrate materials such as lignin.

Structural carbohydrates can't be digested by animals, because these do not

Relationship between plant cell wall and dietary fibre:

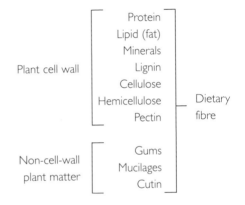

have the digestive enzymes capable of breaking the complex bonds that hold that fibre together. Thus digestion takes place in the hindgut by microbial fermentation, and the end products are substances known as volatile fatty acids, mainly propionic acid, acetic acid and/or butyric acid. These are absorbed from the hindgut into the bloodstream, and are the main energy source for most horses. As the fermentation process takes time, so the release of volatile fatty acids occurs over an extended period. As there is no rush of energy, energy derived from fibre is said to be non-heating.

Hay is an important provider of dietary fibre

Non-Structural Carbohydrates

These are the starches and simple sugars that can be broken down by the horse itself in the small intestine, and the end products of their digestion are sugars that are absorbed from the small intestine. This energy is more rapidly available to the horse, and is often referred to as a 'heating'-type energy, as the rapid increase in energy can make a horse excitable.

Glucose levels in the blood are tightly controlled, which is necessary as glucose represents the preferred form of energy for most tissues. Therefore as it is absorbed into the blood after a meal, so the production of the hormone insulin by the pancreas is triggered. Insulin is an

> ### Lactose
>
> Until very recently it was thought that adult horses were unable to digest lactose, the milk sugar. However, recent research has shown that horses are able to produce the enzyme necessary to break down and utilize milk sugar.

anabolic hormone that encourages the uptake of glucose from the blood into liver and muscle for storage as glycogen, and into adipose cells for storage as fat.

It goes without saying, therefore, that a large meal high in starch and sugar causes a rise in blood glucose with a concomitant rise in insulin shortly after. There is an interesting difference between horses and ponies in the production of insulin after a meal: ponies secrete less insulin than horses do, and the resulting differences in muscle fuel increase that happen (i.e. horses receive more of this 'fuel' into their muscles than ponies do) may explain the difference between the behaviour of horses and ponies after a meal.

STARCH AND SUGAR OVERLOAD

Given that the relatively short small intestine is the only part of the digestive tract where starch and sugar can be digested and absorbed, any that passes through undigested ends up in the hindgut. Once in there it will be broken down by microbial fermentation, and not by the horse's own enzymes. The end product of this fermentation is not volatile

Starch and sugar contents of horse feeds

Feedstuff	Starch % in dry matter	Sugar % in dry matter
Grass	Trace	20–30
Hay	Trace	2
Haylage	Trace	10
Oats	50	2
Barley	60	2
Maize	70	2
Low energy cube	10	7
Low energy mix	25	8
Competition cube	20	7
Competition mix	30	8
Chaff	Trace	12
Molasses	Trace	45
Molassed sugar-beet pulp	Trace	25

fatty acids, but lactic acid. This is a strong acid that, when formed, alters the gut environment, making it more acid. In doing so this can kill the fibre-digesting microbes present, as they cannot tolerate the more acidic fermentation environment.

Even a partial starch or sugar overload can precipitate a disruption to the hindgut fermentation, and as this comprises such a large part of the digestive system, it can have a marked effect on the horse's well-being. Signs of starch overload range from the mild, that is, loose droppings, to the worst, colic and laminitis.

Feeding Strategies

Safe levels of starch to feed: feeding strategies to prevent starch and sugar overload

- ❑ Never feed more than 2kg (4.4lb) of hard feed at a time.
- ❑ Keep starch intakes below 0.25 per cent of body-weight, equivalent to 0.9kg (2lb) of starch per meal.
- ❑ In high risk horses, opt for low starch feeds; cubes are always lower in starch than mixes, and chaffs are lower still.

Flaked maize has a high starch content

Barley is generally used as a conditioner

Heating and Non-Heating Feeds

The effect that energy has on a horse depends largely on its genetic make-up and temperament. Thus for some, feed is fuel injection, but for others no amount of food can provide the necessary motivation for anything active. Feeds that excite horses are commonly said to be heating, and those that don't, non-heating. However, the type of feed, the amount fed, and the time of feeding can all have an effect on behaviour, if there is one to be had.

Diets that are high in starch and sugar can generate a 'heating effect'. Oats, for instance, have their reputation for 'heating up' horses – making them excitable – because their starch is rapidly digested and made available as an energy source – about 85 per cent of an oat starch is digested in the small intestine; this means that the sugars that are the end product of their digestion are readily available soon after a feed. Fibre, on the other hand, is digested more slowly, and the end products of digestion are released more slowly; this results in a constant but steadier flow of energy, and not a sudden rush – hence the term 'non-heating' applied to many high-fibre feeds.

The amount fed also affects the way a horse behaves. If starch or sugar enters the hindgut and causes digestive disturbance, the discomfort may make the horse irascible.

Feeds marketed as 'non-heating' are those that are less likely to produce excitable behaviour in horses and ponies when fed at the manufacturers' recommended rate.

Oats, with their high starch content, have always been viewed as a 'heating' feedstuff

Oils and Fats

Oils and fats are concentrated sources of energy, containing typically two to three times the energy content of the same weight of cereal, and as such are a popular energy source. Generally the term 'fat' is generic for the nutrient, but typically they are distinguished apart in that fats are usually solid, and oils are liquid.

Dietary fats and oils are composed of units called triglycerides, which in turn consist of chains of fatty acids attached to a 'backbone' of glycerol. The fatty acids are further subdivided into essential and non-essential fatty acids, depending on whether the body can make them itself or not. Essential fatty acids are those that the body cannot make, and that must be supplied by the diet.

Horses digest oils in the diet efficiently in the small intestine. It is somewhat of an evolutionary fluke that this is so, since as a forage browser, neat fat in the form of plant lipids would only have accounted for about 2 per cent in the horse's total diet, as compared to humans who adapted to a diet based on a higher proportion of meat.

The horse's ability to metabolize the end products of fat digestion, the fatty acids, is less of a fluke however, as another form of fatty acid, the volatile fatty acid, produced by fibre fermentation, is the main source of energy to the horse. Also the fatty-acid end-products of oil digestion do not precipitate the same increase in blood

> ## Essential Fatty Acids (EFAs)
> **Soya oil, linseed oil** and grass all supply **linolenic acid**, which in addition to its role in the inflammatory response is also used to produce the skin's natural oils. These will therefore promote a shiny coat.
>
> **Corn oil** is a good source of **linoleic acid**, and all **vegetable oils** are equally good as providers of energy.
>
> **Fish oils** and others high in omega-3 and omega-6 fatty acids, such as **evening primrose oil** and **borage oil** or synthetic supplements, are good for combating inflammation, which may explain the old wives' tale of **cod-liver oil** benefiting arthritics.

glucose after a meal, and so do not have the same 'heating effect' of cereals.

In other fibre-fermenters, such as ruminants, feeding high levels of oil has been associated with decreased fibre digestion. However, this does not appear to happen in the horse unless wildly excessive amounts (>20% oil) are fed to horses on low forage diets. Research with oil levels as high as a third of their daily energy intake – equivalent to 1.5kg (3lb 5oz) per day – have not shown this effect.

Oils and fats are more than an energy source, however. Certain fatty acids are involved in general metabolic activity, and some, especially the essential fatty acids (EFAs), are active in the immune and inflammatory responses. Linoleic and linolenic acids are two EFAs, also denoted

Linseed, a rich source of EFAs, in its raw state. Cooked linseed is excellent for promoting a shiny coat

as 'omega 3' (linolenic acid) and 'omega 6' (linoleic acid) fats.

It should be remembered, however, that as oils are energy rich, over-feeding them can lead to weight gain and it must be used with this in mind. Typically adding between 100 and 450g (3.5 and 16oz) per day is plenty for most working horses.

Sources of oil

Source	Oil content %	Typical supply at usual feed rate
Vegetable oil	99	100–200g (3.5–7oz)
High oil compound feed	5–10	200–700g (7oz–1lb 9oz) (depending on feed rate)
Milk pellets	18–20	70–200g (2.5–7oz) (depending on feed rate)
Whole linseed or soya	20–30	200–300g (7–10.5oz) (depending on feed rate)

N.B. No animal fats are included in horse feeds.

Protein

Most of the body consists of proteins in some form, and proteins are essential in the diet too, because of their constituent amino acids, which the body must have in order to synthesize its own internal proteins. Proteins in the body perform a variety of different functions, the main ones being the following:

- ❏ Enzymes are protein molecules that catalyze chemical reactions within the body, such as lactase which breaks down milk sugars.
- ❏ Hormones are the chemical messengers that regulate body processes, such as insulin, involved in glucose metabolism.
- ❏ Structural proteins are those found in muscle and connective tissues, hair and hooves, such as keratin.
- ❏ Immunoproteins or immunoglobulins are produced to fight infection.
- ❏ Transport proteins usually exist within the blood to carry nutrients, such as haemoglobin

There are twenty different amino acids from which all proteins are made, and it is combinations of these that are used to repair and regenerate tissue and other proteins of the body. As with fatty acids, some amino acids are made by the horse itself, while others are not and have to be

Sources of protein		
Feed	Protein content %	Low, medium or high
Spring grass	23–28	High
Autumn grass	14–18	High
Hay	4–8	Low
Lucerne	12–16	Medium-high
Racehorse haylage	4–10	Low-medium
Famer-grown haylage	8–16	Medium-high
Low energy cube or mix (sweet feed)	9–11	Low-medium
Competition feeds	12–14	Medium-high
Racehorse feeds	14	High
Stud feeds	14–18	High
Feed balancers	18	High
Soya	50	High

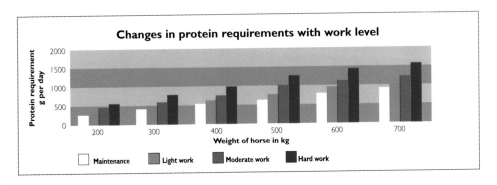

The protein content of compound feeds varies depending on its intended use

supplied by the diet. Those that have to be supplied are known as essential amino acids. All proteins are not equal, however, and depending on the amino acid composition, some are classed as higher quality than others. This is evaluated on how close the amino acids present are to the ratios found in the horse. In horse nutrition the most important amino acids are lysine, threonine and methionine, all essential amino acids, the supply of which is limited in traditional horse diets relative to their role in the body.

Despite the fundamental role of protein as a nutrient, horses, like ourselves, don't need huge concentrations of it in their diets. For horses at rest, the target figure is 8 per cent in the whole diet, and for horses in work it is between 10 and 12 per cent. Proprietary feeds tend to be higher in protein than these requirements, to balance the low supplies from hay. Breeding and youngstock feeds, and those for horses in hard work, tend to be higher in protein than those for horses at rest. These feeds are also significantly higher in energy, and it is often the protein that is blamed if anything goes wrong with horses fed such feeds, rather than the energy content, which is in fact more likely to be to blame.

The main food constituents, their common sources, and the method and end products of digestion

Energy source	Fibre	Starch and sugar	Fat	Protein
Common feed source	Hay, haylage, sugar-beet pulp	Oats, barley, maize Spring grass, molasses	Vegetable oil	Soya bean meal, linseed
Site of absorption	Large intestine	Preferred Small intestine / Accidental Large intestine	Small intestine	Small intestine*
Method of digestion	Fermentation	Enzymes / Fermentation	Enzymes	Enzymes
End product of digestion	Volatile fatty acids (acetic, butyric and propionic acids)	Sugars / Lactic acid	Fatty acids, glycerol	Amino acids
What happens next?	Acetic and butyric acids used in tissues for aerobic energy or stored as fat; propionic acid converted to glucose in the liver	Converted to glucose. Used for aerobic and anaerobic energy; or stored as glycogen in liver and muscles; excess is converted to fat / Drops the pH of the hindgut, causing the death of fibre-fermenting microbes, thereby causing disruption to the gut's fibre-fermenting ability	Fatty acids are used for aerobic energy production in tissues, or the excess is stored as fat. Glycerol is converted to glucose in the liver	Used for protein and essential amino acid synthesis. Excess is broken down: nitrogen is excreted as urea, and carbohydrate is part-converted to glucose.

*Any protein escaping digestion in the small intestine and entering the hindgut will be broken down by the microbes there.

Horses on a natural grass-only diet rich in sugar, protein and fibre

Minerals

Micronutrients are just as their name suggests: nutrients required and used in minute amounts. Their role is to facilitate many of the body's internal reactions, and to do so, supplies of grammes, milligrammes, or fractions of milligrammes per day are required; in other words, very, very small quantities indeed.

There are two types of minerals: major minerals, needed in relatively large quantities, ie grams per day; and trace elements, needed in tiny quantities, milligrams or fractions of milligrams per day. The major minerals are calcium, phosphorous, magnesium, potassium and sodium. There are many trace elements known to man, but the main ones significant in horse nutrition are copper, zinc, manganese, selenium and iron. 99 per cent of all the body calcium is in

Calcium and Phosphorus

the bones and teeth; 85 per cent of the phosphorus is found in bone, and the rest is found in the soft tissues. Both are essential in many body functions, from bone design to nerve and muscle function, cell structure, blood and energy transfer. Both are important to growing horses, as most of the bone is laid down in the first year of life. Calcium is important in the athletic horse – specific types of tying up are linked to calcium metabolism, not through a specific dietary deficiency, but

related to calcium losses in sweat, or an individual horse's genetic inability to metabolize calcium effectively.

With the huge 'reservoir' in bone, the majority of horses are highly adept at maintaining blood calcium levels. When blood calcium levels drop due to exercise or lack of dietary supply, less is excreted through the urine, and when blood calcium increases or is plentiful, these mechanisms are turned off.

Calcium and phosphorus should always be fed in the correct relation one to

---

Calcium and phosphorus

Sources

❑ Grass and grass products supply most of the calcium and phosphorus in the diet, and in the right ratio to each other (2:1).

❑ Alfalfa is calcium rich, with five times as much calcium as phosphorus.

❑ Compound feeds are supplemented with both calcium and phosphorus, typically supplying 10–12g/kg calcium and 6g/kg phosphorus.

Requirements:

❑ A 500kg (1,100lb) horse needs about 25g (0.9oz) of calcium in its diet per day, and about 17g (0.6oz) of phosphorus.

❑ A horse eating 6kg (13lb 4oz) of hay and 4kg (8lb 13oz) of a competition mix, will be receiving 75g (2.6oz) and 45g (1.6oz) of calcium and phosphorus respectively – the excess doesn't matter, but the ratio to each other does: in this example the ratio is correct.

Lucerne: a good source of calcium

another. The ideal is 2:1, especially in breeding horses and youngstock, and in adult exercising horses a ration of a minimum 1:1, but preferably 1.5:1 calcium to phosphorus should be fed.

Magnesium

55 per cent of the horse's magnesium is found in bone, with the remainder in muscles, other tissues and extracellular fluids. Magnesium is also an electrolyte,

---

Magnesium
Sources
- ❏ Green feeds are rich sources, as chlorophyll contains magnesium.
- ❏ Compound feeds contain 0.15–0.2 per cent magnesium.
- ❏ Molasses and sugar-beet pulp are useful dietary additions, with good levels of magnesium.

Requirements:
- ❏ Magnesium is required at 0.1 per cent of the diet.

---

but it is also functional in energy generation and transfer, DNA and protein manufacture. It is rarely deficient in horse diets in the UK, but is most likely in horses on low forage, high grain diets. There are also claims that megadoses of magnesium can effectively calm horses with excitable tendencies.

Sodium

Sodium together with chloride makes up salt, which is one of the major electrolytes.

Electrolytes are defined as electrically charged versions of major minerals or compounds that exist in the plasma of the blood and in the fluids that occur in and between cells. They all facilitate nerve and muscle function, and they are important because they are lost together with fluid when a horse sweats.

Sodium and chloride are the main electrolytes of the extracellular fluid (that surrounds the individual cells of the body). Extracellular fluid is lost when a horse sweats, which is why sweat tastes salty.

Loss of electrolytes *per se* affects performance by affecting muscle function and the amount of enthusiasm a horse has for its work, but as they can only exist in water, either in blood plasma or elsewhere in the body, water is important, too. Electrolyte loss occurs almost incidentally when there is a loss of water, through sweat for example.

Electrolyte Facts

The main electrolytes in the body are sodium, chloride, potassium, calcium and magnesium. Bicarbonates, phosphates and sulphates can also play electrolyte roles.

Fluid losses of 10–15ltr (2.2–3.3gal) per hour can be achieved in high stress conditions, but more typically will be in the region of between 1 and 5ltr (0.2–1.1gal) for a sharp gallop, and 8ltr (1.8gal) for an endurance horse.

Electrolytes
Daily supplies
- Forage supplies high amounts of calcium, phosphorus and potassium. The fibre in forage also binds water into it in the digestive tract, which acts as an internal fluid and electrolyte reservoir.
- Add salt daily, either as a salt lick or adding it to the feed in 1–2 tablespoons per day to top up dietary levels. Forages are sometimes low in sodium, and so additional salt in the diet ensures that requirements are met.
- When rehydrating horses, in order to speed recovery from strenuous exercise and improve the horse's ability to cope with stress, it is essential to replenish lost fluid and electrolytes, together with sugar, either as glucose or a glucose-type compound, as this facilitates electrolyte absorption from the gut.

As electrolytes are soluble in water, and their concentrations in the body are under continuous control, any dietary excesses are excreted in the urine.

Copper

Copper is involved in many internal functions of the horse: in the manufacture of bone and cartilage; as one of a group of nutrients that acts as antioxidants; in the transfer of iron; and in the production of a variety of hormones.

Copper has gained the importance it has mainly due to its role in cartilage formation. Copper has a vital role in the development of bone, and a deficiency can affect bone development, particularly in those breeds with a genetic predisposition to grow fast, such as Thoroughbreds and Warmbloods. However, despite heavy supplementation of copper in these horses, bone developmental diseases have not disappeared, underlining the multifaceted aetiologies of such conditions.

Some British soils, particularly in the western half of the country, are notoriously

Copper
Sources
- Grass and forages: contain 4–9mg/kg, depending on the area.
- Compound feeds: usually supplemented with between 10 and 40mg per kg.

Requirements
- Horses need between 10 and 30mg of copper per kg of the diet – the lower level for working horses and the higher level for mares and growing youngstock. Excess copper is not poisonous: a horse merely shuts off absorption of the copper it doesn't need.

low in copper, and horses receiving mainly forage diets in these areas could be copper deficient. Signs of deficiency are more easily seen in ruminants, commonly appearing as ill-thrift in lambs, or discolored coats in cattle. There are anecdotal reports of coat discoloration in copper-deficient horses.

Iron

Iron has almost mythological status in horse nutrition – a stalwart of ancient feed-room potions, it was often thought of as a blood booster (a category of supplements also known as hemanitics). Iron is best known as part of red blood cells, and the classic symptom of iron

Mares and youngstock require some minerals at higher levels than other horses

deficiency is anaemia, although this sort of deficiency is very rare in the horse. Iron is a critical component of haemoglobin, the special protein that carries oxygen in the blood. Iron deficiency slows the production of haemoglobin and red blood cells, in turn causing anaemia. Like the other trace elements, it is also involved in many enzyme systems, and in immune system function.

The horse is very efficient in its use of iron, and so examples where anaemia, as indicated by low serum ferritin, could occur are:

- ❑ in chronic illness (which affects red cell production in the bone marrow);
- ❑ in haemorrhage (acute or chronic – gastric ulcers are thought to be a contributor to long, slow, red blood-cell loss);
- ❑ after viral illness, as iron is metabolized by the stimulated immune system;
- ❑ and there is also evidence from human athletes that the iron requirements of those in heavy stress increase as a result of red blood cell damage through concussive sport, and it is reasonable to expect the same to be true of the horse.

Very few studies have examined the effectiveness of iron supplements on performance, but those that have done have observed no effect. Iron is so rarely limiting in the diet, it is likely that the increased requirements of horses in work are met by the increased intakes of supplementary feeds.

Zinc

This is a crucially important trace element, integral as a co-factor in over 200 enzyme systems in the whole body. It is particularly important in protein and carbohydrate metabolism, and for connective tissue development. Any deficiencies depress appetite and growth rate, and affect skin and coat quality, but are very rare. Excessive amounts of zinc can cause a copper deficiency.

Zinc occurs naturally in many feed ingredients, and is usually supplemented in proprietary feeds and supplements.

Zinc
Requirements
- ❑ 50mg/kg of the diet.

Manganese

Another trace element involved in many body processes, manganese is essential in carbohydrate and lipid metabolism, and also in the synthesis of the endogenous glycosaminoglycan – chondroitin sulphate in the joints, which is part of the cartilage formation process. It also acts as an antioxidant, as a free-radical scavenger.

Iron
Sources
- ❑ Iron is plentiful in all forages and is usually added to proprietary feeds.

Requirements
- ❑ The adult horse requires 40mg/kg and foals and youngstock 50mg/kg.

Manganese is usually found above the required levels in the diets of horses. It is usually added to proprietary feeds and supplements, and forage is also a rich source.

Manganese
Requirements
- ❏ 50mg/kg of the diet.

Cobalt

A lesser known trace element, used as a constituent of vitamin B12, and rarely deficient in equine diets. Together with vitamin B12, it is involved in blood-cell formation and nervous system function.

Cobalt
Requirements
- ❏ 0.1mg/kg of the diet.

Iodine

This is another trace element required in acutely trace quantities. Iodine is integral in the production of thyroid hormones, and therefore plays an important role in the regulation of metabolic rate. The thyroid hormones also play a role in the maturation of bone in growing horses.

Iodine deficiency and excess are rare, and both are manifest by the appearance of goitre, enlargement of the thyroid gland.

Iodine
Requirements
- ❏ 0.1mg/kg of the diet.

Selenium

Selenium is a trace element most often identified for its role as an antioxidant working in conjunction with vitamin E. It is an essential part of the enzyme glutathione peroxidase, a key enzyme in the body's antioxidant defences. Selenium has equally important but lesser known roles in iodine metabolism, the repair of DNA, and also in the immune system, although this latter role may be linked to its antioxidant properties.

Selenium
Sources
- ❏ Soils in the UK are generally low in selenium, and so therefore are the plants, forages and cereals grown from them. Proprietary feedstuffs are usually supplemented with selenium, either as sodium selenite or as organic or chelated selenium.

Requirements
- ❏ Horses require 0.15mg of selenium per kg of feed.

Toxicity:
- ❏ Selenium is rare amongst the micronutrients in that it is toxic at the relatively low level of ten times requirement. Outside Britain there are areas where soil and therefore plant selenium concentrations are high, and there are also certain plants that can 'accumulate' selenium, such as milk vetch, woody aster and goldenweed. Signs of toxicity include the loss of mane and tail hair, the sloughing off of hooves, lameness and leg deformities in foals.

Antioxidants

Many trace elements and certain vitamins are known to exert antioxidant properties, and the role of this important group of nutrients in cellular defence is worthy of further examination. Antioxidants are a 'buzz' word in human and animal nutrition, offering protection against cancer, ageing and stress.

Antioxidants act to 'scavenge' free radicals that cause damage to cells. Free radicals are meteor-like, unstable oxygen molecules that oxidize and destabilize tissues that they come into contact with. They are produced by a number of normal metabolic processes in the body, such as energy production, liver function and immune system attack, but issues arise when the level of free radical production, through overexertion, disease challenge, radiation and poor nutrition, exceeds the body's ability to contain them.

All the components of tissues are susceptible to free radical damage, but lipids (body fats) and proteins are particularly affected, and disruption of these affects cell function completely, and this in turn affects resistance to stress and disease.

Nutrients that act as antioxidants are vitamins A, C and E, and beta carotene, together with the trace elements, notably selenium, manganese and zinc. Each works in a different way within the body. Vitamin E 'fields' the free radicals, whereas selenium works to prevent their formation in the first place.

Natural antioxidants occur in plants, and if you think about it, this is quite logical, as plants are exposed to radiation from the sun on a daily basis, and would need inbuilt antioxidant defences. Natural antioxidants are found in all coloured plants, as flavonoids, bioflavonoids, flavones, proanthocyanidins and finally hesperidins.

As the nutrients that act as antioxidants cannot be manufactured by the horse, their only supply is via the diet. For horses at grass, and those that receive compound feeds and broad-spectrum supplements, there will be an ongoing supply of the antioxidant nutrients available, but for hay- or haylage-fed horses on a diet of straights such as oats and bran, the supply of these will be reduced, as none of those feeds contains appreciable amounts of vitamins or trace elements.

Fat breakdown can also occur in feedstuffs containing high levels of oil; such breakdown is known as rancidity. Antioxidants are therefore used in foods and feeds to prevent this occurring.

In horse feed, only certain antioxidants are allowed, and these are seen on the label as BHT or BHA, added to protect the oils and vitamins in the feed.

A broad range of minerals are available from grazing

Typical mineral concentrations in grass and grass products and their relationship to a horse's requirement

Mineral	Content per kg	Daily requirement
Calcium	3–10g	circa 25g (500kg horse)
Phosphorus	1.5–4.5g	circa 17g (500kg horse)
Magnesium	1–3g	11g (500kg horse)
Sodium	1–6g	1–3g/kg
Potassium	15–45g	
Copper	2–15g	10-15mg/kg (growing horses, 30mg)
Manganese	25–250g	40mg/kg
Zinc	20–60mg	40mg/kg
Iron	100–170mg	40mg/kg (lactating mares, 50mg)
Selenium	0.01–0.15mg	0.1mg/kg

Vitamins

These are non-mineral substances required in minute quantities in the diet to maintain health and normal bodily functions. The main vitamins are the fat-soluble vitamins, A, D, E, K; and the water-soluble vitamins, vitamin C, and those that comprise the B vitamins.

Vitamin A

Also known as retinol, one of the four fat-soluble vitamins. In nature, this vitamin is only found in animal products, and so the horse obtains its vitamin A from converting β-carotene found in green herbage into vitamin A. It has been estimated that this process is inefficient, most likely an evolutionary development designed to protect the horse from vitamin A toxicity.

Proprietary feeds and supplements contain additional vitamin A, so that the field-kept horse, or one receiving compound feeds or supplements, should receive in excess of requirements. In fact, vitamin A toxicity is more likely in modern feeding than deficiency, as vitamin A is liberally added to some products. A classic sign of oversupply of vitamin A is loss of appetite.

Apart from grazing, good sources of β-carotene are legumes such as clover. Hay and other conserved forages are poor sources.

Vitamin D

This vitamin is required for the maintenance of calcium and phosphorus levels in the horse. It is manufactured in the skin on exposure to sunlight, and stored in the liver. Additionally, it is commonly supplemented in compound feeds and supplements.

Deficiency of vitamin D is rare in horses, and is manifest as rickets.

Both vitamins A and D are naturally accumulated by the horse during the summer months, but if unsupplemented once the horse is removed from pasture, or in the winter when there is little sun, liver stores will be depleted.

Vitamin E

Also known as α-tocopherol, vitamin E acts as an antioxidant, and as such fulfils an important role, firstly in the diets of exercising horses, where the resulting additional stress increases free radical production, and secondly, in support of normal immune function.

The classic deficiency sign is muscle degeneration or 'white muscle disease'.

Good sources are fresh green forages and the germs of cereals, and most feedstuffs contain ample supplementation of this vitamin. Cereals, especially those rolled or processed in any way, and forages contain little vitamin E.

Increasing the fat content of a horse's diet increases its requirement for vitamin E, as these extra lipids in the body are as susceptible to damage from free radicals as body lipids.

High levels of vitamin E are also said to have a calmative effect on horses.

Vitamin K

This vitamin, like the B-vitamins, is synthesized in the hindgut by the micro-organisms there, and is not generally ever considered deficient, unless prolonged and sever hindgut disruption takes place.

It is essential in the blood-clotting process.

Vitamin C

This water-soluble vitamin is readily synthesized by the horse from glucose. Functioning as an antioxidant, the requirement for vitamin C increases as a horse is exposed to any kind of stress. It has been suggested that in exercising horses, the requirement for vitamin C outpaces the body's ability to manufacture it. However, this has not been scientifically proven, and moreover, supplementary forms of vitamin C are poorly absorbed, and are also destroyed by heat in feed-manufacturing processes.

Vitamin safety levels

All the water-soluble vitamins can be fed safely at high levels; that surplus to requirements is excreted in the urine.

B-Group Vitamins

These water-soluble vitamins are manufactured in the body by the fermentation process in the hindgut, and horses receiving adequate amounts of forage are usually B-vitamin sufficient. The main B-vitamins are B1 (thiamine), B2 (riboflavin), B6 (pyridoxine), niacin, pantothenic acid, folic acid, biotin, and vitamin B12.

All are involved in energy transfer within the body. In addition, biotin has been shown at levels far greater than are usually added in feed, to be beneficial in promoting hoof quality in horses. Levels of 15–20mg per day have proved effective against weak, cracked hooves when fed over an extended period.

Physiology in Perspective

To know the dimensions of the digestive tract and the nutrients supplied by the food so digested, does not complete the subject of nutrition. The use of nutrients by the body in relation to performance, be it in exercise or growth, completes the picture.

Nutrition is often the poor relation when the success or otherwise of equine endeavour is discussed, although the feed is often the first area put under scrutiny when things go wrong. The role of nutrition is important in performance success, alongside other factors of equal or greater significance:

- ❑ **Genetics:** no amount of feeding can overcome genetic superiority or weakness.
- ❑ **Conformation:** poor conformation affects movement, soundness and the ability of the horse to perform optimally.
- ❑ **Attitude:** even with the best genetics and conformation, a horse's temperament and attitude determine its ability to withstand work.
- ❑ **Training:** training both in fitness and skill, of the horse and of the rider, affects athletic performance.

As with human athletes, correct nutrition is one of the keys to good performance

Exercise Physiology

It is beyond the remit of this book to provide a treatise on exercise physiology, and this section is limited to investigating energy generation in the muscles to fuel movement.

Once absorbed, nutrients need to be effective at fuelling the muscle fibres to generate movement. Contraction of the muscle fibres is fuelled by a chemical called ATP (adenosine triphosphate), and the rate of use of ATP by the muscles depends on the rate of contraction of the muscle fibres. Muscle stores very limited amounts of ATP, and therefore mechanisms exist to generate it as needed. ATP is generated in two ways:

❑ aerobically, a relatively slow series of chemical reactions using oxygen; or

❑ anaerobically, a fast but inefficient method used in the absence of oxygen.

Muscle Fibre Types

As with feed fibre, there is more than one kind of muscle fibre, and these differ according to the speed of contraction of the individual fibre type, and whether it generates ATP aerobically or anaerobically. There are three types of muscle fibre:

❑ **Type I:** contract relatively slowly, and are known as 'slow twitch'; they generate energy aerobically, and are engaged at low speeds.

❑ **Type IIA and Type IIB:** contract quickly, and are known as 'fast-twitch' fibres. Type IIA can generate energy aerobically and anaerobically, and the process of training or physical conditioning promotes their use. Type IIB fibres generate energy anaerobically.

The characteristics of these fibres are as follows:

	Type I	Type IIA	Type IIB
Speed of contraction	Slow	Fast	Fast
Power generated	Low	High	High
Types of work	Walking	Trot, canter, speeds up to 26mph (42km/h)	Galloping, jumping, power work

At high speed, 'fast twitch' fibres contract quickly generating massive amounts of motive power

The importance of this relative to nutrition is that each fibre can use a different energy source.

Type I muscle fibres can use fatty acids as the energy source by which ATP is generated, as can Type IIA fibres. Both type IIA and IIB utilize carbohydrate, either as glucose or its stored form glycogen.

Fatty acids that are the end product of fibre digestion, and free fatty acids that are the end products of oil digestion, can therefore act as fuel for types I and IIA muscle fibres. When adding oil to diets, it is recommended that the oil is added at least six weeks before the competition season commences. The physiological significance of this is that it allows the type IIA fibres to adapt to its use and to generate ATP aerobically.

Glucose and its storage form, glycogen, can be used by all muscle fibre types, but are essential for type IIB fibres, and therefore for fuelling fast work, jumping efforts or any other power work.

Feeding strategies to ensure there is enough glucose and glycogen for anaerobic energy production when required, revolve around 'sparing' its use in muscles by encouraging the use of oil as an energy source, either from dietary fibre or oil.

Growth Physiology

The phenomenon of growth in young horses is worthy of comment, especially compared to that which human babies achieve. At birth, the foal is typically 10 per cent of its adult mature weight, as compared to a baby at 5 per cent. At the end of its first year a foal will have achieved 60 per cent of its adult weight, 90 per cent of its adult height, and 95 per cent of its adult bone growth, although there will always be exceptions and differences between colts and fillies. Again, as compared to human babies (10–12 per cent of weight, 33 per cent of height in year one), this is incredibly fast, and requires supreme metabolic effort and a serious nutrition supply.

Typical weight gains in fast-growing and native breeds (kg per day)

	Thoroughbreds/ Warmbloods	Native breeds
Foals	0.5–1	0.3
Weanlings	0.3–0.7	0.2
Yearlings	0.2–0.4	0.1

Growth is fastest during the spring and summer when diets are based on grass, and slower in the winter, when animals are on forage-based diets.

It goes without saying that bone is laid down first, as this provides the framework (skeleton) on which all else develops. Muscle-fibre types are heritable, and are laid down in the first twenty-four months.

Bone grows by the elongation of each end of the long bones, in an area known as the growth plate. Here, cartilage is laid down and then subsequently converted to bone. It is in this conversion that many developmental bone diseases have their basis.

An enormous cocktail of nutrients is required for growth in this way, as energy to fuel the process, and protein and minerals to make the conversion. Besides calcium and phosphorus, copper, zinc and manganese are all involved in the conversion of cartilage to bone; however, modern thinking suggests that the hormonal environment created by the supply of energy also plays a significant role in bone development.

It has been demonstrated that high blood glucose concentrations from starch as an energy source, results in high blood insulin concentrations, and that this in turn reduces thyroid hormone concentrations. A reduction in these reduces the maturation of cartilage into bone, with resulting effects on bone quality. Sourcing energy from forage or controlled starch diets promotes a hormonal environment more conducive to perfect maturation and growth of bone.

In the first year of its growth a foal will have gained a massive 90% of its adult height

GLOSSARY

Acute Sudden in onset.

Alfalfa *Medicago sativa*, also known as lucerne, or legume forage or common hay in the US. More frequently used as a chaff or ingredient of compound feeds in Europe. Medium energy, high protein and high calcium.

Allergies Rapid onset immune system related exaggerated response to a substance, with which it comes in contact, usually a protein. Rare in horses, often mistaken for food intolerances. See p128.

Amino acids Component parts of protein. There are over 20 different amino acids, nine (histidine, isoleucine, leucine, lysine, methionine, phenylalanine, threonine, tryptophan and valine) are classified as essential, i.e. dietary supply is essential. Lysine, threonine and methionine considered the most important.

Antioxidants General term applied to compounds and trace elements that perform a role preventing free radical damage within the body.

Anti-nutritional factors Naturally occurring substances in common feedstuffs that either prevent absorption (e.g. anti-trypsin factor in raw soya) or can cause illness or death. (Hydrocyanic acid in linseed.)

Azoturia See ERS.

B-group vitamins A group of water-soluble compounds measured in minute quantities and involved in the main in energy transfer. Produced naturally by hindgut microbes and commonly added to compound feeds. Main B-group vitamins are B1 (Thiamine) B2 (Riboflavin) B6 (pyridoxine), Nicotinic acid, B12, Folic acid, Pantothenic acid, Biotin.

Beta carotene One of the yellow plant pigments, best known for contributing to the colour of carrots. Some conversion of beta-carotene to vitamin A takes place within the digestive tract.

Biotin B vitamin responsible for many functions in the body, including energy metabolism. Proven to improve hoof quality at 15mg per day.

Botulism Disease often inaccurately linked to haylage, caused by *Clostridium botulinum* toxin that causes rapid death by paralysis. *C. botulinum* found in wet poorly fermented silages, soil and decomposing animal tissue.

Vitamin C Water soluble vitamin. Acts as antioxidant manufactured by the horse from glucose. Production may not meet demand under high stress and external sources may be beneficial.

Calcium Major mineral, important component of bones teeth and essential for growth and nerve and muscle function.

Carbohydrates Compounds comprised of combinations carbon, hydrogen and oxygen. Subdivided into non-structural (starch and sugars) and structural (fibre) carbohydrates.

Cellulose Structural complex carbohydrate of plant cells. One of the components of fibre.

Cereals Traditional, high starch, energy ingredients of horse diets. Oats, barley and maize (corn) are most widely used although wheat is also included in some feeds to a lesser extent.

Chelation Chelated minerals (sometimes referred to as organic minerals) are minerals that have been chemically bound to carbohydrates or amino acids. Proven to increase their availability via alternative routes of absorption.

Chondroitin sulphate Component of joint cartilage. Often used in joint supplements with in conjunction with MSM and glucosamine. Thought to act by decreasing activity of destructive joint enzymes.

Chronic Of long duration.

Compound feed Balanced blends of straights and other ingredients formulated to produce a complete ration when fed in conjunction with forage. Designed as complete (can be fed as whole diet) or complementary (designed to be fed in conjunction with forage). Supplements are technically complementary compound feeding stuffs.

COPD Chronic Obstructive Pulmonary Disease. Now known as Recurrent Airway Obstruction (RAO).

Crib-biting (cribbing) Stereotypical behaviour involving habitual swallowing of air by horse while biting on solid object.

Vitamin D Fat-soluble vitamin, synthesised by the horse in sunlight.

Developmental Orthopeadic Diseases Umbrella term for variety of bone disorders of growing horses related to diet and genetic predisposition such as osteochondrosis.

Digestion Process by which feedstuffs are broken down and absorbed within the body.

Vitamin E Fat-soluble vitamin. Important antioxidant.

Echinacea Herb proven to improve immune function.

Electrolytes Minerals and mineral salts (sodium,

potassium, magnesium and chloride) present in the body's fluids. Responsible for conducting electrical impulses for muscle contraction. Responsible also for internal water balance. Most horses normally receive required amount of electrolytes, except sodium, in their feed. Adding 1–2 tablespoons of salt daily to the feed or allow free access to a salt lick is often advised. Horses competing and travelling regularly should receive electrolytes to replace those lost through sweat. Use in the feed, water or syringed.

Energy value Measure of the potential a feed or foodstuff to provide fuel for body processes. Measured in the UK in units of Megajoules per kilogramme (MJ/kg), and in the US as mega calories per pound (Mcal/lb).

Epsom salts Common name for magnesium sulphate, added as a purgative to diets, particularly bran mashes.

Extruded Form of feed processing, more often used in dry dog food manufacture. Feed passes through small shaped openings under high pressure and on exit, the rapid release of pressure causes the feed to expand.

Fibre Structural carbohydrate component of the diet. Commonly measured in feeds as crude fibre, although more accurate characterisation of fibre via alternative analysis, Neutral Detergent Fibre (NDF) and Acid Detergent Fibre (ADF) also available.

Folic acid See B-group vitamins.

Forage Anything that makes up the bulk fibre component of the diet: grass, hay, haylage, commercially prepared hay-replacers.

Free radicals Dangerous electrons produced within cells in response to stress that cause damage to cell membranes and therefore function. Antioxidants are the defence mechanism against free radicals.

Fructans Non-structural storage carbohydrates currently the focus of research into the causes of laminitis. Found in grass. Under certain climatic conditions can reach very high concentrations in grass.

Fructo-oligosaccharides See prebiotics.

Glucose: Fundamental monosaccharide sugar molecule; one of few energy sources used by the brain. Created as end product of starch digestion, often referred to as instant energy. If unused immediately for energy, glucose can be stored as glycogen or converted and stored as fat, a process controlled by the hormone insulin.

Glucosamine Complex sugar forming the 'backbone' of glycosaminoglycans, (components of cartilage and connective tissue). Involved in repair of cartilage damage. Also used in the body's own synthesis of chondroitin sulphate.

Glycogen Storage form of carbohydrate in muscles and liver.

Hay Common horse forage, available in seed, meadow and legume varieties.

Haylage Increasingly popular forage of horses in Europe, consisting of semi-moist, baled and wrapped grass that has undergone a limited fermentation.

Hemicellulose Component of fibre comprising variety of complex carbohydrates. Indigestible by enzymes, fermented in the large intestine.

Heating Refers to the effect feed has on a horse, in that horses become hot headed after ingesting certain feedstuffs e.g. oats.

Iron Trace element, found in abundance in most feedstuffs. Deficiency in horses is rare, but manifests as anaemia.

Vitamin K Fat-soluble vitamin, synthesised by the horse, and essential for blood clotting.

Lactic acid Weak organic acid. Occurs variously as the active acid in the preservation of haylage, the end product of cellular anaerobic respiration that causes muscle fatigue, and the end product of the unwelcome fermentation of cereal in the large intestine.

Lactose Disaccharide milk sugar. Horses were thought to lose any ability to digest lactose after about 4 years of age; recent research has suggested they remain able to breakdown lactose well into later life.

Laminitis Painful inflammation of the laminae of the feet. Also known as founder.

Lignin Non-carbohydrate, indigestible component of fibre.

Linoleic and linolenic acid Essential fatty acid (i.e. must be supplied in diet).

Lysine Most important essential amino acid.

Magnesium Major element required for blood haemoglobin, muscle and enzyme function, and bone formation. Naturally occurs in many feedstuffs.

Malabsorption Failure of horse to digest or absorb nutrients, usually the result of illness.

Manganese Trace element with antioxidant properties.

Mannan Oligosaccharides See prebiotics.

Micronising Process used to cook cereals to make the starch in them more digestible. Commonly used on barley, maize and peas, which when subsequently flaked are used in coarse mixtures.

Micronutrients The word 'micronutrient' simply describes the nutrients needed in the diet only in very small amounts such as vitamins and trace elements for example selenium, iron, copper etc.

Molasses Commonly added sweetener, by-product of sugar production from sugar cane or sugar beet.

MSM Abbreviated name for Methyl Sulphonyl Malonate a sulphur-containing sugar and source of organic sulphur. MSM is often included in joint supplements for these reasons as well as some hoof preparations.

Mycotoxins Term covering a wide variety of toxic metabolites of moulds, produced under certain conditions if mould is 'stressed' during growth.

Nicotinic acid One of the B-group vitamins.

Osteochondrosis One of the developmental bone diseases.

Oxalates Constituents of certain subtropical plants that irreversibly bind calcium and render it inaccessible to the horse.

pH Indicator of the acidity or alkalinity of a feed on a scale of 1 (very acid) to 14 (very alkaline).

Pantothenic acid One of the B-group vitamins.

Peas Protein and starch rich legume used to add these nutrients and colour to coarse mixtures (sweet feeds).

Pellets Form of extrusion process that produces cubes, nuts or pellets. Also forces feed mixture through a die as with extrusion, but under less pressure. Pellets are more dense than extruded feeds.

Phosphorus Major element important in bone formation and energy transfer as adenosine triphospate (ATP).

Potassium Major element and electrolyte found in great abundance in forages.

Prebiotic Complex sugars that act to stimulate the growth of beneficial bacteria in the gut, either by the supply of a fermentable food source in the case of fructo-oligosaccharides (FOS), or by acting to remove harmful bacteria (pathogens) by binding irreversibly to them (mannan-oligosaccharides). Garlic is also often described as having prebiotic properties.

Probiotic Preparations of live bacteria that can be fed to add beneficial bacteria, i.e. naturally occurring bacteria that can aid digestion, to the horses digestive system. They work by competing and excluding pathogenic bacteria that could cause disease if allowed to flourish there. As their name suggests, probiotics have the opposite effect of antibiotics (which kill harmful bacteria). Under feed legislation, yeasts are classed as probiotics, although they work in a different way.

Protein Complex molecules comprising linked chains of amino acids used in various bodily structures and functions.

Salt Sodium chloride, an important electrolyte.

Selenium Mineral trace element that works very closely with vitamin E to protect the muscles from damage during exercise. Deficient in the soil in many areas of the UK; certain plants of the USA accumulate selenium. A low excess is highly toxic.

Starch and sugar Non-structural carbohydrates digested mainly in the small intestine by digestive enzymes and broken down to glucose.

Steam flaking Another way of processing cereals to cook the starch. Instead of using microwaves this process uses steam, which cooks the starch in the grain again causing it to gelatinise. The cooked grains are then rolled and cooled making flaked barley, maize and peas.

Straights Cereals, cereal by-products (such as bran), proteins (e.g. soya) and other primary processed unfortified feedstuffs, including sugar beet pulp.

Straw By-product of the harvesting of cereals. Low energy, high fibre material used as a forage, a feed ingredient and as bedding.

Sulphur Major mineral critical in the formation of collagen and other connective and structural proteins.

Theobromine Prohibited substance under FEI and Jockey Club rules; found in tea, coffee, cocoa containing materials.

Trypsin Protein digesting enzyme of the small intestine. Inhibited by some anti-nutritional factors in uncooked or processed soya.

Tryptophan One of the essential amino acids, best known for its role in the production of serotonin, a brain neurotransmitter involved in sleep promotion and mood. Often included in calming supplements.

Vitamins Group of organic compounds occurring in food that are essential for normal metabolism. Divided into fat soluble (vitamins A, D E and K) and water soluble (vitamin C, B-group vitamins)

Volatile Fatty Acids (VFAs) End-product of microbial breakdown of fibre in the large intestine. Principal VFAs are propionic, acetic and butyric acid. They are absorbed into the bloodstream and constitute a major energy source for the horse.

Weaning Process of removing foal from mare and onto a diet of solids. Weaning causes a mare to cease milk production. Stress of weaning is associated with development of stereotypical behaviours in some foals.

Windsucking See crib-biting.

Wood chewing Habit of horses related to boredom or gastric acidity.

Yeasts See probiotics.

Zinc Essential trace element.

USEFUL ADDRESSES

UNITED KINGDOM
British Equestrian Federation
NAC, Stoneleigh Park, Kenilworth, Warks CV8 2RH
www.bef.co.uk
British Horse Society
Stoneleigh Deer Park, Kenilworth, Warwickshire
CV8 2XZ
www.bhs.org.uk
British Equestrian Trade Association (BETA)
Stockeld Park, Wetherby, West Yorkshire LS22 4AW
www.beta-uk.org
British Equine Veterinary Association (BEVA)
Wakefield House, 46 High Street, Sawston,
Cambridgeshire CB2 4BG
www.beva.org.uk
DEFRA
Room 311, 10 Whitehall Place, London SW1A 2HH
Direct Laboratories Ltd
Woodthorne, Wergs Road, Wolverhampton
WV6 8TQ
Food Standards Agency
Room 424, Aviation House, 125 Kingsway, London
WC2B 6NH
www.foodstandards.gov.uk
Spillers
Old Wolverton Road, Old Wolverton, Milton Keynes
MK12 5PZ
www.spillers-feeds.com

Worshipful Company of Farriers
22 Church Street, Romsey, Hampshire SO51 8BU

NORTH AMERICA
American Farrier's Association
4059 Iron Works Pkwy, Suite 1, Lexington KY40511
USA
American Medical Equestrian Association
PO Box 130848, Birmingham, AL 35213-0848
USA
American Veterinary Medical Association
1931 North Meacham Road, Suite 100, Schaumburg
IL 60173, USA
Canadian Veterinary Medical Association
339 Booth Street, Ottawa, Ontario K1R 7K1
Canada
Saddle, Harness and Allied Trades Association
1101-A Broad Street, Oriental, NC 28571
USA

AUSTRALIA & NEW ZEALAND
Australian Veterinary Association
PO Box 371, Artarmon, NSW 1570
Australia
New Zealand Veterinary Association
PO Box 11–212, Manners Street, Wellington
New Zealand

CONVERSION TABLE

In these quick-reference conversions the figures have been rounded up or down.

Weight conversions

ounces to grams multiply by 28.3494
grams to ounces multiply by 0.0353
pounds to kilograms multiply by 0.4536
kilograms to pounds multiply by 2.2046

oz	g	g	oz	lbs	kg	kg	lbs
1oz	28g	15g	½oz	1lb	0.45kg	1kg	2.2lb
2oz	56g	20g	¾oz	2lb	0.90kg	2kg	4.4lb
3oz	85g	30g	1oz	3lb	1.40kg	3kg	6.6lb
4oz	113g	5g	1¼oz	4lb	1.80kg		
5oz	142g	40g	1½oz	5lb	2.25kg		
		45g	1½oz				

Fluid conversions

fluid ounces to millilitres multiply by 28.4
millilitres to fluid ounces multiply by 0.3519
pints to litres multiply by 0.5682
litres to pints multiply by 1.7598

fl oz	litres	ml	fl oz	pt	litres	litres	pt
2fl/oz	57ml	10ml	3½fl/oz	1pt	0.5l	1l	2pt
4fl/oz	114ml	20ml	7fl/oz	2pt	1l	2l	3½pt
6fl/oz	170ml	30ml	10½fl/oz	3pt	1.5l	3l	5pt
8fl/oz	227ml	40ml	14fl/oz	4pt	2.25l	4l	7pt
10fl/oz	280ml	50ml	17½fl/oz	5pt	3l	5l	8¾pt
20fl/oz	560ml			10pt	5.5l		

INDEX

Page numbers in *italic* refer to picture captions

acetic acid 151, 160
adenosine triphosphate (ATP) 174–5
aerobic conditioning 86
age of horse 81
alfalfa 18, 34, *34*, 162
    compound feeds 44
allergies and intolerances 128–9, 138–9
amino acids 107, 158–9, 160
anaemia 166
antacids 126
antibiotics 105
antioxidants 71, 88, 96, 166, 167, 168, 170, 171
anus *13*
appetite loss 127
apples *48*, 49
Arabs 57, 110
arsenic 72
aspartate amniotransferase (AST) 115
Aspergillus fumigatus 29, 138
autumn 79, 82, 106
azoturia 122

back: pain 85, *114*; stiff 11
balancers 18, 42, 65, 108, 158
barley 36, 37, 108, 129, *153*, 160
    boiled *37*; bruised *37*; feed value 41, 152; flaked 37; micronized 37; whole *37*
barley straw 33
bedding: allergic reaction to 129; mites 129
best before date 71
beta carotene 168
BHA 168
BHT 168
bicarbonates 164
bile 134
biotin 171
bit, poorly fitting 85
black walnut 67
blood 158
    glucose level 152; hemanitics 165; iron content and anaemia 165–6; tests 115, *115*, 127, 134
bones 176
botulism 30, 32
box-resting horses 104–5
box-walking 14
bracken 67
bran 38, *38*, 142–3
    feed value 41, 142–3; mash 38, 105, 142
breathing 138–9
brood mares 92–5
    retained placenta 118
BSE 71
bucking 11
bullies 62
buttercups 24, 67
butyric acid 151, 160

caecum *13*

caffeine 72
calcium 38, 39, 130, 142–3, 162–3, 164, 169, 170
calming supplements 84, 171
calories 148
carbohydrates 150–5
    complex 150; non-structural 152–3; structural 150–1
carrots *48*, 49
    water content 20
cartilage 176
cellulose 90, 150
cereals 36–7, *36*, *37*, 129, 142–3
    compound feeds 44; older horses 91
chaffs 18, 34, 133
    alfalfa 34, *34*, forage blends 34; grass 34; measuring 60; molassed 34, *34*; ponies 83; sugar content 152
changing diet 55
    buying a new horse 80–1; colic 117
chewing 10, *10*, *11*, 12, 126
chilling a horse 117
chloride 163–4
choke 133
chondroitin sulphate 49
chops 34, *34*, 133
    measuring 60
chronic obstructive pulmonary disease (COPD) 29, 83, 138–9
Clostridium botulinum see botulism
clover 170
coarse mixtures 18, 42, *43*, 129
    measuring 60, 65; water content 20
coat 158
    condition 40, 47; curly 120, *120*; discoloration 165
cobalt 167
cobs 57, 110
colic 10, 60, 91, 116–17, *153*
    gas 117; impaction 116, 117; sand 117; spasmodic 117; symptoms 116
colon *13*
colostrum 100
competition feeds 42, 148, 152
competition horses: feeding guidelines 58, 68, 86–9; gastric ulcers 126; oil supplements 47
compound feeds 42–5, *42*, *43*, *63*; high oil 157; least cost formulation 45; measuring 60
concentrates 14, 55
concussive exercise 166
condition of horse 55, 56, 81, 127
conditioning feeds 107, 108, *153*

conformation 172
copper 33, 130, 162, 164–5, 166, 169
cortisone 118
coughing 138
creatine kinase (CK) 115
crib-biting 14, 136, *137*
cubes 18, 42–5, 129
    competition 148; low energy 42, 148, 152; measuring 60, 65; older horses 91; racehorse 42; water content 20
Cushing's disease 90, 91, 118, 120–1

Dartmoor ponies 57
dehydration 88, 146, 164
developmental orthopaedic diseases (DODs) 130–1
DHA 47
difficult keepers see poor doers
digestive aids 50–1, 105
digestive system 8–15, 55, 126, 160
    enzymes 14, 15, 160; evolution 6, 8, 12, 14, 156; large intestine *13*, 14, 15; microbial fermentation 14, 15, 50–1, 106, 151, 160; mouth 10–11; small intestine 12, *13*, 15; stomach 12, *13*
disaccharides 150
docks 24
domestication 8
dope testing 72
dressage 58, 86
drooling 132
droppings: clearing pasture 25, 26; loose 153
drought 66
duodenum 15
dust 28, 29, 33, 55, 83, 103, 138–9
dysphagia see choke

easy keepers see good doers
electrolytes 49, 65, 79, 163–4
    competition horses 88; racehorses 102; sweating 124; testing status 115
endurance 58, 86
energy supply 148–9; heating and non-heating feeds 151, 152, 154
enzymes 14, 15, 158, 160, 167
EPA 47
equine rhabdomyolosis syndrome (ERS) 122–5
    chronic 122, 124; sporadic 122, 124, 125
essential fatty acids (EFAs) 156
establishment's number 71
eventing 58
excitability 84–5

heating feeds 154
exercise and feeding 55, 58, 60–1, 65, 68
    competition horses 58, 68, 86–9; water 146
exercise physiology 174–5
exertional myoglobinuria 122
exertional rhabdomyolosis 122
eyesight, checking 85

fail-safe diet 80
farmer's lung 29
fats 156–7, 171
    digestion 160
fatty acids 15, 47, 151, 156–7, 160, 175
feed management 64–7
feed room equipment 64
feeding position, natural 10–11, *11*, 62, *63*, 133
feeding principles 55–8, 80–1
    calculating basic ration 58, 60–1; choosing a product 74; exercise levels 55, 58, 60–1, 65, 68; fail-safe diet 80; timing feeds 62–3
FEI rules 72
fevers 118, 129
fibre 36, 39, 55, 175
    bran 142–3; carbohydrates 150–4; compound feeds 42, 45; cubes 42; digestion 14, 15, 160; gastric ulcers 126; heating and non-heating feeds 154; non-heating energy 151; older horses 90
fibre mixes 18
first turn-out 66
fish oils 47
flaking 37, *37*, 129
foals: choke 133; developmental orthopaedic diseases (DODs) 130–1; growth physiology 176–7; orphaned 100–1
folic acid 171
forage 10, 14, 18, 22–35, 108, 126
    ad libitum basis 62–3, *114*; analysis 35; feeding guidelines 61; natural feeding position 62, *63*; poisonous plants 66–7; ponies 83; racehorses 103; and water intake 65
    see also grass; hay; haylage; pasture; traw
forage blends 34
foxgloves 67
free radicals 88, 166, 168
fructan theory 119, 121
fructo-oligosaccharides (FOS) 51
fruit 49

gas colic 117

gastric ulcers 12, 126–7
genetically modified
  organisms (GMOs) 45
genetics 172
gestation 92
glucosamine 49
glucose 152, 160, 164, 175
glycerol 157
glycogen 160, 175
goitre 167
good doers 56, 110
grain mites 64
grass 18, 22–7
  colic 117; compound feeds
  44; energy content 148,
  149; feed value 22, 33, *162*;
  fructan theory 119, 121;
  hours at grass 23; laminitis
  22, 27, 79, 118–21, 141;
  mineral content 169;
  mixed grazing *23*; oils 47;
  poisonous plants 66–7,
  134; ponies 83; protein
  content 22, 158; starch
  content 152, 160; sugar
  content 22, 140–1, 152,
  160; water content 20, 33;
  weight loss regime 110–11
  see also pasture
green feeds 163, 170
growth: ailments associated
  with 130–1, 164;
  physiology 176–7

haemoglobin 158, 166
haemorrhages 166
hard feet 46
hay 15, 28–9, 106
  ad libitum basis 114;
  allergic reaction to 129,
  138–9; big-bale 9; dust
  content 28, 29, 38–9;
  energy content 148; feed
  value 33, 162; fibre
  content *151*, 160;
  meadow 28, *29*, 33;
  measuring 60, 65; moulds
  138–9; older horses 90;
  ponies 83; protein content
  158; seed 28, 29, 33;
  soaking 28, 139, *139*;
  starch content 152;
  storage 28, 29; sugar
  content 152; water
  content 20, 33
haylage 15, 28, 29, 30, *31*, 79
  analysis 35; energy content
  148; feed value 33; fibre
  content 160; measuring
  60; protein content 158;
  soaking 139; starch
  content 152; storage 30;
  sugar content 152; water
  content 20, 33, 79
haynets 10, *11*
head pressing 134
head tossing 11
heating and non-heating
  feeds 151, 152, 154
heavy horses 49, 57
helplines, feed 74
hemanitics 165
hemicellulose 90, 150
hemlock 66, 67
herbs 50, 72, 84

hindgut 14
hives 128–9, *128*
hooves *118*, 158
  cracked 171; hoof
  supplements 49
hormones 158
horse tail (plant) 67
horse-sick pasture 22, 24, 46
humidity 146
hunters 57
hunting 58
hydrocortisone 72
hygiene 64, *64*
hyperadrenocorticism *see*
  Cushing's disease

identity preserved (IP) 45
ileum 15
immune system 100, 120,
  156
immunoglobulins 158
immunoproteins 158
impaction colic 116, 117
incisors 10, *12*
inflammation 47, 156
inflammatory airway disease
  (IAD) 138
insulin 65, 152, 158
intestines 12, *13*, 14–15, 134,
  160
iodine 167
Irish draught horses 110
Irish sport horses 57
iron 33, 127, 162, 165–6, 169
irritability 127
ISO9002 standard 74

jaundice 134
jejunum 15
Jockey Club rules 72
joints 45, 166
  osteochondritis dissecans
  (OCD) 130
joules 148
jumping 118, 126

keratin 158

labels, feed 70–1
lactase 158
lactating mares 56, *56*, 92–5
lactic acid 32, 157
lameness 114
  fructan theory 119, 121
laminitis 22, 27, 60, 79, 91, 96,
  118–21, 141, 153
  Cushing's disease 90, 91,
  118, 120–1
large intestine *13*, 14, 15, 160
lawns and roughs 22
least cost formulation 45
legumes 170
lignin 90, 150
limestone 38, 39, 143
linoleic acid 156
linolenic acid 47, 156
linseed 40, *40*, 41, 108, 157,
  157, 160
  feed value 41; mash 40; oil
  47
lips 10
liver *13*, 160
  disease or damage to
  134–5; ragwort 134, *134*
livery, keeping at 81

low energy feeds 42, 148,
  152, 158
lucerne 158, *163*
lusine 159

magnesium 84, 129, 162, 163,
  164, 169
maize 36–7, 160
  feed value 41, 152, *153*;
  flaked 37, *37*, *153*;
  genetically modified (GM)
  45; identity preserved (IP)
  45
manganese 33, 130, 162,
  166–7, 168, 169
mangolds 49
manic walking 134
mannan-oligosaccharides
  (MOS) 51
mare's tail (plant) 67
meadow hay 28, *29*, 33
melatonin 92
methionine 159
methyl sulphonyl malonate
  (MSM) 47
microbal fermentation 14,
  15, 50–1, 106, 151, 160
micronizing 37, 37, 40
micronutrients 162
Micropolypora faeni 138
milk pellets 108, 157
milk replacers 101
minerals 15, 20, 162–9
  compound feeds 45; feed
  storage 64; forage analysis
  35; forage feed values 33;
  straights feed values 41;
  supplements 49
mixed grazing *23*
molars 10, *12*
molassed chaffs 34, *34*
molasses 18, 39, 129, 152,
  160, 163
  compound feeds 44
Monday morning disease 122
monosaccharides 150
morphine 72
moulds 29, 30, 33, 35, 55,
  138–9
mouth 10–11
mueslis 18
muscles 115, 158
  development 107; equine
  rhabdomyolysis syndrome
  (ERS) 122–5; fibre types
  174–5; white muscle
  disease 170

nasal discharge 138
native ponies 56, 57, 82–3,
  99, 110, 118
nettles 25
New Forest ponies 57
niacin 171
nutraceuticals 49–50
nuts *44*

oak 67
oat straw 33
oatfeed 15
oats 36–7, 102, 160
  energy content 148, *149*,
  154, *155*; feed value 41,
  152; rolled 36, *36*; water
  content 20; whole *36*

obesity 22, 56, 110–11, 119
oesophageal impaction *see*
  choke
oesophagus *12*
oils 47, 156–7, 160, 175
  digestion 15, 160; energy
  content 148; linseed 40;
  measuring 60
older horses 90–1
omega 3 fats 156
omega 6 fats 156
opium poppies 72
orphaned foals 100–1
osteochondritis dissecans
  (OCD) 130
ovulation 92

pain relief 50
pantothenic acid 171
parsnips 48
pasture 22–7
  active improvement 26;
  clearing droppings *25*, 26;
  drainage 24; horse-sick 22,
  24, 46; laminitis 22, 27, 79,
  118–21, 141; lawns and
  roughs 22; management
  24–7; overgrazed 66;
  poaching 24, 26; rolling 24;
  under-grazing 24–5; weeds
  22, 24–5, 26, 66–7, 134
  see also grass
pathogenic bacteria 51
pelleted feeds 133
performance 114–15
performance boosters 143
phosphates 164
phosphorus 15, 38, 90, 130,
  143, 162–3, 169, 170
photosensitivity 134
physiology 172
  exercise 174–5; growth
  176–7
pituitary pars intermedia
  dysfunction (PPID) *see*
  Cushing's disease
placenta, retained 118
poaching 24, 26
poisonous plants 66–7, 134
police horses 58
pollen 139
polysaccharide storage
  myopathy (PSSM) 122,
  124–5
polysaccharides 150
ponies 82–3
poor doers 39, 56
potassium 162, 164, 169
potatoes 48, 49
prebiotics 50–1
pregnancy 92–5
premolars 10, *12*
probiotics 50
prohibited substances 72
propionic acid 151, 160
protein 107, 150, 158–9,
  160
  allergic reaction to 128–9;
  compound feeds 45;
  digestion 15, 160; grass 22,
  158, 160; linseed 40
pulse 116
pyridoxine 171

Quarter Horses 124, *124*

quidding 10, 91

racehorse cubes 42
racehorses 58, 102–3
    prohibited substances 72
ragwort 25, 66, 66, 67, 134
rectum 13
recurrent airway obstruction
    138–9
recurrent equine
    rhabdomyolosis syndrome
    (RER) 122–5
respiratory allergy (RAD) 60,
    83
respiratory system 114
retching 132
retinol 170
riboflavin 171
rickets 170
ringworm 129
rolling 116, 116
roughage 33, 34, 55
routine, importance of 6, 55,
    62–3
rug, poorly fitting 85
rug-chewing 14
ruminants 14, 165

St John's wort 67, 84
salicylic acid 72
saliva 10, 12, 126, 133
    regurgitation 132, 132
salt 163–4, 165
sand colic 117
seed hay 28, 29, 33
selenium 33, 88, 162, 167,
    168, 169
setfast 122
Shire horses 57
show horses 58, 86
    weight requirements 109
show jumping 58, 86
silage 30, 32, 32, 33
small intestine 12, 13, 134,
    160
sodium 162, 163–4, 169
solar prolapse 118
soya: compound feeds 15; full
    fat 40, 41, 157; oils 47;
    protein content 158, 160
spasmodic colic 117
spleen 13
spring 79, 106
    laminitis 118–21; ponies
    82

stabled horses 62–3, 81,
    136–7
    exercise 116; water supply
    20
stallions 68, 96
starch 130, 150–4
    cereals 36–7; digestion 15,
    160; heating and non-
    heating feeds 154;
    overload 152–3
stereotypical behaviours
    136–7
stomach 12, 13
    gastric ulcers 12, 126–7
stomach acid 12, 14, 126
storage 28, 29, 30, 64
straights 18, 36–41
    feed values 41
straw: allergic reaction to
    129; as forage 18, 33, 90
stress 14, 89, 171
    laminitis 118
stud horses 68, 96, 158
succulents 48–9, 48
suckling reflex 100
sugar 140–1, 150–4
    digestion 15, 160;
    electrolyte absorption
    164; grass 22, 140–1, 160;
    overload 152–3
sugar-beet pulp 36, 39, 41,
    163
    compound feeds 44;
    energy content 148; feed
    value 41; fibre content
    160; molassed 152; soaked
    39, 39, 133; unsoaked 39,
    39; water content 20
sulphates 164
summer 79, 82, 106
sunflower meal 15
supplements 18, 46–7, 49
    calming 84
sweating 88, 102
    colic 116, 117; Cushing's
    disease 120; electrolyte
    loss 163–4; equine
    rhabdomyolosis syndrome
    (ERS) 122, 124
swedes 48, 49
sweet feeds see coarse
    mixtures

tack, poorly fitting 85
teeth 10–11, 12, 46, 62, 63,

81, 106, 114
    choke 133; dental hygiene
    10–11; excitable horses
    85; feeding position
    10–11, 11; hooks 10, 11,
    11; impaction colic 116,
    117; older horses 91;
    tooth loss 10
temperament of horse 55,
    56, 81, 86, 172
    excitable horses 84–5
testosterone 72
theobromine 72
Thermophilic actinomyces
    138
thiabendazole 118
thiamine 171
thistles 24
Thoroughbreds 57, 98, 130,
    164
threonine 159
thyroid hormones 167
timing feeds 62–3, 65
toxaemia 118
toys 49, 136
training 172
travelling 88, 146
treats 18, 51, 136
triglycerdes 156
trytophan 84
turnips 48, 49
tying up 60, 122

UKASTA Feed Assurance
    Scheme 74
ulcers, gastric 12, 126–7
urea 160
urine: discoloured 122; tests
    115
urticaria 128–9, 128

valerian 72, 84
vegetables 49
vices 136–7
viral infections 129, 166
vitamins 168, 170–1
    A 15, 33, 96, 168, 170;
    B group 15, 50, 167, 170,
    171; C 168, 170, 171;
    D 15, 170; E 15, 33, 84, 88,
    96, 167, 168, 170–1;
    K 170, 171; box-resting
    horses 104–5; compound
    feeds 45; feed storage 64;
    forage feed values 33;

straights feed values 41;
    supplements 49

Warmbloods 57, 98, 130,
    164
waste products 88, 134
water, digestion 15, 65
water supply 20, 21, 55, 86,
    146–7
    chemical analysis 146; colic
    117; competition horses
    88; hay in diet 29; haylage
    in diet 20, 33, 79; poor
    drinkers 146; succulents
    49; water content of
    feedstuffs 20
weanlings 99, 100, 176
weaving 136
weeds 22, 24–5, 26, 66–7,
    134
weigh tapes 57, 57
weight of horse 55, 56
    feeding guidelines 57,
    60–1; feeding to gain
    weight 106–9; feeding to
    lose weight 22, 56,
    110–11; measuring 57;
    seasonal fluctuation 106
weight loss 134
Welsh ponies 57
wheat 38, 129
wheat straw 33
wheatfeed 15
white muscle disease 170
wind-sucking 136
winter 79, 106
    laminitis 119; out-wintering
    81, 82, 106; ponies 82
wood shavings 67
work levels, feeding
    guidelines 55, 58, 60–1, 68
worming 46, 91, 106, 116,
    117, 118

yawning 134
yearlings 176
yeasts 50, 105
yew 66, 67
youngstock 66, 98–9
    choke 133; developmental
    orthopaedic diseases
    (DODs) 130–1

zinc 33, 130, 162, 166, 168,
    169

ACKNOWLEDGEMENTS

All photographs by Kit Houghton except:
pp 19, 54, 57, 75 **Spillers**
p32 **David & Charles**
pp 56, 96–7 **David & Charles/Phot: Bob Atkins**
pp 62–3, 90–1 **David & Charles/Phot: Bob Langrish**
    (Courtesy Amanda Sutton)
pp80–1 **David & Charles/Phot: Kit Houghton**
pp84–5 **David & Charles/Phot: Matthew Roberts**
pp 94–5, 100–1, 124, 131, 142, 177 **Bob Langrish**

p114 **David & Charles/Phot: Andy Perkins**
p115 **Andrew Carter**
pp 116, 132 **Tony Pavord**
p128 **Dr Derek Knottenbelt**/University of Liverpool Dept
    of Veterinary Clinical Science and Husbandry

Artworks
pp 10, 11 **David & Charles/Maggie Raynor**
pp12–13 **David & Charles/Paul Bale (Visual Image)**